STUDIES IN ECONOMIC AND SOCIAL HISTORY

This series, specially commissioned by the Economic History Society, provides a guide to the current interpretations of the key themes of economic history, in which advances have recently been made, or in which there has been significant debate.

The series will give readers access to the best work done, help them to draw their own conclusions in some major fields and, by means of the critical bibliography in each book, guide them in the selection of further reading. The aim is to provide a springboard to further work rather than a set of pre-packaged conclusions or short cuts.

ECONOMIC HISTORY SOCIETY

The Economic History Society, which numbers over 3,000 members, publishes the *Economic History Review* four times a year (free to members) and holds an annual conference. Inquiries about membership should be addressed to the Assistant Secretary, Economic History Society, Peterhouse, Cambridge. Full-time students may join the Society at special rates.

STUDIES IN ECONOMIC AND SOCIAL HISTORY

Edited for the Economic History Society by M. W. Flinn

PUBLISHED

B. W. E. Alford Depression and Recovery? British Economic Growth, 1918–1939

S. D. Chapman The Cotton Industry in the Industrial Revolution

R. A. Church The Great Victorian Boom, 1850–1873

D. C. Coleman Industry in Tudor and Stuart England

P. L. Cottrell British Overseas Investment in the Nineteenth Century

Ralph Davis English Overseas Trade, 1500–1700

M. E. Falkus The Industrialisation of Russia, 1700–1914

M. W. Flinn British Population Growth, 1700–1850

John Hatcher Plague, Population and the English Economy, 1348–1530

J. R. Hay The Origins of the Liberal Welfare Reforms, 1906–1914

R. H. Hilton The Decline of Serfdom in Medieval England

E. L. Jones The Development of English Agriculture, 1815–1873

John Lovell British Trade Unions, 1875–1933

J. D. Marshall The Old Poor Law, 1795–1834

Alan S. Milward The Economic Effects of the Two World Wars on Britain

G. E. Mingay Enclosure and the Small Farmer in the Age of the Industrial Revolution

A. E. Musson British Trade Unions, 1800–1875

R. B. Outhwaite Inflation in Tudor and Early Stuart England

P. L. Payne British Entrepreneurship in the Nineteenth Century

Michael E. Rose The Relief of Poverty, 1834–1914

S. B. Saul The Myth of the Great Depression, 1873–1896

Arthur J. Taylor Laissez-faire and State Intervention in Nineteenth-century Britain

Peter Temin Causal Factors in American Economic Growth in the Nineteenth Century

OTHER TITLES ARE IN PREPARATION

Laissez-faire and State Intervention in Nineteenth-century Britain

Prepared for
The Economic History Society by

ARTHUR J. TAYLOR

Professor of Modern History
in the University of Leeds

First edition 1972
Reprinted 1974, 1977

Published by
THE MACMILLAN PRESS LTD
London and Basingstoke
Associated companies in Delhi Dublin
Hong Kong Johannesburg Lagos Melbourne
New York Singapore and Tokyo

ISBN 0 333 09925 7

Printed in Hong Kong by
CHINA TRANSLATION & PRINTING SERVICES LTD

Contents

Acknowledgements

THE bibliography stands as a statement of my wide indebtedness, but I should like to express particular thanks to Professor A. W. Coats, who guided me to writings in his own field which I might otherwise have overlooked, and to Professor M. W. Flinn, an ever-helpful and indulgent editor.

The title of this study is borrowed without permission from J. B. Brebner's 1948 essay which was the starting-point for many of the controversies which it has been my purpose to examine.

A.J.T.

Editor's Preface

SO long as the study of economic history was confined to only a small group at a few universities, its literature was not prolific and its few specialists had no great problem in keeping abreast of the work of their colleagues. Even in the 1930s there were only two journals devoted exclusively to this field. But the high quality of the work of the economic historians during the inter-war period and the post-war growth in the study of the social sciences sparked off an immense expansion in the study of economic history after the Second World War. There was a great expansion of research and many new journals were launched, some specialising in branches of the subject like transport, business or agricultural history. Most significantly, economic history began to be studied as an aspect of history in its own right in schools. As a consequence, the examining boards began to offer papers in economic history at all levels, while textbooks specifically designed for the school market began to be published.

For those engaged in research and writing this period of rapid expansion of economic history studies has been an exciting, if rather breathless one. For the larger numbers, however, labouring in the outfield of the schools and colleges of further education, the excitement of the explosion of research has been tempered by frustration caused by its vast quantity and, frequently, its controversial character. Nor, it must be admitted, has the ability or willingness of the academic economic historians to generalise and summarise marched in step with their enthusiasm for research.

The greatest problems of interpretation and generalisation have tended to gather round a handful of principal themes in economic history. It is, indeed, a tribute to the sound sense of economic historians that they have continued to dedicate their energies, however inconclusively, to the solution of these key problems. The results of this activity, however, much of it stored away in a wide range of academic journals, have tended to remain inaccessible to many of those currently interested in the subject. Recognising the need for guidance through the burgeoning and confusing literature that has grown around these basic topics, the Economic History Society decided to launch this series of small books. The books are intended to serve as guides to current interpretations in important fields of economic history in which important advances have recently been made, or in which there has recently been some significant debate. Each book aims to survey recent work, to indicate the full scope of the particular problem as it has been opened up by recent scholarship, and to draw such conclusions as seem warranted, given the present state of knowledge and understanding. The authors will often be at pains to point out where, in their view, because of a lack of information or inadequate research, they believe it is premature to attempt to draw firm conclusions. While authors will not hesitate to review recent and older work critically, the books are not intended to serve as vehicles for their own specialist views : the aim is to provide a balanced summary rather than an exposition of the author's own viewpoint. Each book will include a descriptive bibliography.

In this way the series aims to give all those interested in economic history at a serious level access to recent scholarship in some major fields. Above all, the aim is to help the reader to draw his own conclusions, and to guide him in the selection of further reading as a means to this end, rather than to present him with a set of pre-packaged conclusions.

M. W. FLINN
Editor

It was the age of Samuel Smiles and the self-made man, of the dominance of the *bourgeoisie*. Its political foundations were the general abstention of the State from attempts to control the course of industrial development and the reliance on the initiative and unrestricted competition of independent business concerns. It was the age of *laissez-faire*.

Britain's Industrial Future (The Liberal Yellow Book) (1928) p. 6

I do not myself think that the conception of a period of *laissez-faire* is helpful. It has just enough truth to conceal its defects, which are many, and it is an encouragement to error.

G. S. R. KITSON CLARK, *An Expanding Society: Britain, 1830–1900* (1967) p. 162

'When *I* use a word,' Humpty Dumpty said in rather a scornful tone, 'it means what I choose it to mean, neither more nor less.'

LEWIS CARROLL, *Through the Looking-Glass*

1 Towards a Definition of Laissez-faire

THE consideration of a subject so contentious as *laissez-faire* should properly begin with a definition of the term itself. Unlike mercantilism, with which it has frequently been contrasted, *laissez-faire* was a term current in the period to which it has been most commonly applied. Its French origins lie deep in the eighteenth century and it was mentioned by Lord Liverpool in the House of Lords as early as 1812. Before the middle of the nineteenth century, however, references to *Laissez-faire* in literature or debate are relatively infrequent. Like many terms familiar to the historian - Medievalism, Renaissance and the Industrial Revolution are obvious examples - *laissez-faire* was a term more honoured by use in later generations than in the period to which it has closest reference.

Time which extends the use of words also widens their meaning. Few of those who have used the term *laissez-faire* in the present century have troubled to define it. Its meaning, therefore, can only be inferred. There are some who would appear to equate *laissez-faire* with anarchy. Others, notably Carlyle and Spencer, have indentified it with 'anarchy and the constable' or the 'negatively regulative' state. At the other extreme are those who use *laissez-faire* to mean no more than a preference for private rather than public enterprise. More frequently, *laissez-faire* has been used as a convenient shorthand for the general prescriptions of the Classical economists and in particular for a belief in the efficacy of a free market economy. In a more precise form it has been regarded as synonymous with free trade - the more so when free trade is extended, as it was in the nineteenth century, to cover the markets in land and labour as well as in goods.[2]

This variety also shows itself in the areas to which the term is applied. While some, with early usage and the authority of the *Shorter Oxford English Dictionary* to support them, restrict the use of *laissez-faire* to economic questions, there are those who place an equal emphasis on social policy and others who extend their use of the term to embrace the entire field of governmental action. Similarly, a distinction can be made between the use of

11

laissez-faire to differentiate private from corporate action, whether the action be undertaken by the state itself or by a local authority, and its employment to distinguish specific state action from action taken by any lesser body, whether private or public. Thus, while some have regarded the concern for public health shown by local authorities in early Victorian England as a movement away from *laissez-faire* towards collectivism, others have viewed the resistance of these same authorities to the centralising tendencies of the General Board of Health as a no less striking manifestation of the operation of the *laissez-faire* principle.

Given these variations in definition, it is hardly surprising that one man's *laissez-faire* is another man's intervention. The removal of the restrictions on workers' combinations in 1824 has been represented by some as an example of *laissez-faire* in that it conceded the right of working men to combine in the pursuit of their common economic ambitions; others have seen it as an interference with the free contractual relationship between master and man on which the normal operation of the labour market is based. In the same way the joint-stock legislation of 1825–62 has been viewed both as emancipatory in removing restrictions on the mobility of capital and as interventionist in according privileges to corporate enterprises which were denied to the individual entrepreneur. Nor is this ambiguity simply a problem created by historians. While Cobden attacked the land laws in the name of free trade, nineteenth-century landowners invoked *laissez-faire* in their defence.

Advantageous as it might therefore be to establish initially a firm definition of *laissez-faire,* to do so would be to remove an important underlying element from the consideration of the debate. The question of terminology is one to which it will be necessary to return, but in the meantime the debate must be approached by a different route.[3]

2 The Area of Debate

THIRTY years ago the place of the state in the nineteenth-century British economy was a subject presenting few problems to the student of economic history. The few textbooks available to the undergraduate offered interpretations notable for their unanimity, and the learned journals were largely empty of controversy. The nineteenth century was viewed as an age dominated, as least until its final quarter, by the principle and practice of *laissez-faire,* expressed in terms both of economic ideas and of social policy. 'The less government intervention there was in any sphere the better.'[4]

This interpretation of the part played by government in the nineteenth-century economy can be expressed in a series of propositions:

(i) In the first three-quarters of the century British public life was strongly influenced by the complementary ideologies of the Classical economists and the Benthamite Utilitarians who were at one in preaching the virtues of economic individualism.

(ii) The ideas of the Classical economists and the Utilitarians harmonised with the needs and aspirations of the ascendant middle classes. Through the thought and activity of the Manchester School and of the propagandist agencies associated with it, these ideas worked powerfully in shaping the policies of government.

(iii) The influence of *laissez-faire* ideology was most powerful in the economic sphere; but it was also strong in social policy. Where, as in the case of the Factory Acts, there were apparent contraventions of the *laissez-faire* principle, these were limited and to be justified in terms of John Stuart Mill's dictum that 'every departure from *laissez-faire, unless required by some great good,* is a certain evil'[5] (my italics). Though, therefore, the pressures of industrialisation and urbanisation occasioned some admitted divergences from *laissez-faire,* belief in the general efficacy of the principle remained undisturbed for at least a generation after 1850.

(iv) Only after about 1870 did the strong tide of *laissez-faire* begin to ebb in face of changes in theory, anticipated in part by John Stuart Mill but made more positive by W. S. Jevons; and, more compulsively, in response to increasing doubts felt by industrialists, merchants and politicians about the wisdom of non-interventionist policies in the economic field, and to new sentiments, even more widely held, about the nature of society and social policy.

During the past thirty years each of these propositions has been subjected to question and challenge. The war of arguments which has filled the journals for more than two decades has had no common theme except that the disputants have been concerned with the subject of *laissez-faire* and state intervention. Whereas in other debates – that over the standard of living, for example – the field of conflict can be readily defined and the combatants no less clearly identified, in the controversy about *laissez-faire* there are many battle-fronts, and political and administrative as well as economic and social historians fight out their own private wars. It is essential, therefore, at the outset to survey the broad field of debate and to identify the principal theatres of discussion and controversy.

At a fundamental level there has been intensive argument in recent years about the theory of economic policy as it is seen to have developed in the work of the British Classical economists. This subject has engaged the attention of many distinguished scholars in Britain and America and has been productive both of wide-ranging general assessments and of more detailed studies of the thinking and writing of individual economists. Less attention has been paid to the means by which the ideas of the Classical economists reached a wider audience and the form in which they were received by society at large. This is a subject of particular interest and importance to the student of economic policy and involves on the one hand consideration of the writings of popularisers of economic thought like Mrs Marcet and Harriet Martineau and of the contributors to journals like the London *Economist*, and on the other evaluation of the part played by Classical economic thinking in shaping the activities of the Manchester School and other movements for reform which flourished in the middle decades of the nineteenth century. Although there has been distinguished work in this area, it lies relatively thinly on the academic ground, and even less attention has been given to systematic investigation of the impact of Classical economic thinking on politicians as revealed in the records of parliamentary debate.

By contrast, it is arguable that disproportionate attention has been given to discussion of the relationship between Classical political economy and Utilitarianism. Early (i.e. pre-1939) economic historians experienced little difficulty in synthesising the two movements of ideas. 'The political economists were Benthamites', asserted C. R. Fay.[6] Equally, in his view, Bentham was a Classical economist and a follower in particular of Malthus and James Mill. 'Under his influence *laissez-faire* held the field in English industry and commerce for the greater part of a century.'[7] It would be difficult to find anyone disposed to speak in such unqualified terms today. In recent years Bentham's place among the Classical economists has been a matter of much discussion, his commitment to *laissez-faire* has been severely questioned, the content of his social theory has been similarly scrutinised and his influence on public policy has been strenuously debated. It is this last topic which has particularly engaged the interest and passion of administrative historians and, as a by-product, has brought forth discussion of other schools of thought which developed in response to the needs of nineteenth-century society.

But while much energy has been applied to the consideration of the intellectual background of economic and social policy, the major focal point of debate has necessarily been the activity of government itself. Where Lillian Knowles, following faithfully in the tradition of her great tutor Cunningham, characterised the first three-quarters of the nineteenth century as an era of almost unqualified *laissez-faire*, David Roberts has discerned in the same period the origins of the Welfare State.[8] The two views are not logically irreconcilable, but an examination of their detailed development reveals an unbridgeable gulf of evidence and interpretation. The gap, however, is not necessarily one of two different generations. Within the last decade Eric Hobsbawm has affirmed that 'the history of government economic policy and theory since the Industrial Revolution is essentially that of the rise and fall of *laissez-faire*', and that 'by the middle of the nineteenth century government policy in Britain came as near *laissez-faire* as has ever been practicable in a modern state'.[9]

In the debate on the prevalence or otherwise of *laissez-faire* and the nature and extent of government intervention, historians have cast their nets widely. From the works of Holdsworth, Brebner and Kitson Clark, for example, it is possible to draw up an extensive list of governmental *acta* in the economic and social fields ranging from the registration of marriage to the authorisation of joint-stock companies. Debate, however, has tended to concentrate on certain major fields: on free trade and fiscal policy; on railway legislation; on the Poor Law and the factory question; and on the development of the Civil Service and its influence on the economics of government. There have also been substantial investigations of emigration and of policy towards Ireland, neither of which was conspicuously the subject of contemporary ideological controversy, but both of which throw an interesting retrospective light on ideas and practice relating to state activity.[10]

Out of this many-sided controversy has emerged the overall question: was this an age of *laissez-faire*? In common with the majority of earlier historians – and not uniquely even among those of his own generation – Hobsbawm would clearly offer an affirmative answer. By contrast, there are many who would accept the view of Kitson Clark that the concept of a period of *laissez-faire* is 'not helpful to the historian'.[11]

Directly related to the notion of an age of *laissez-faire* is the question of its chronology. Even among those who have most readily embraced the concept there have been many who have accorded *laissez-faire* only a short period of dominance. Some have dated its passing from the 1830s with the coming of the first major Factory Act and the beginning of urban administrative reform; others have seen the high tide of *laissez-faire* as reached and passed at the middle of the century with the achievement of free trade in corn and the repeal of the Navigation Laws. A more generally held view is that the decline of *laissez-faire* set in from the 1870s when the advent of the Great Depression and the rise of labour coincided with new trends in economic and social thinking. But there are those who see the influence of *laissez-faire* stretching down into the twentieth century and yielding only gradually to collectivist counter-pressures. In this particular area

16

of debate, as elsewhere in the general controversy, definition and the viewpoint of the observer are no less significant than the facts of the case.

In this essay consideration will be given in turn to each of these major areas of discussion and argument. A broad division will be made between thought and policy, and in each instance the first concern will be to present the arguments of the 'revisionist' school which have made the running in recent debate. Thereafter in each major section an attempt will be made to reassess the older 'traditionalist' view in the light of the evidence and arguments of the revisionists. Finally, the validity of the concept of an 'age of *laissez-faire*' will be tested.

3 The Theory of Economic Policy

'*LAISSEZ-FAIRE* has never been preached as an absolute dogma by any English economist.'[12] Though few, if any, historians of economic thought can be found to disagree with this view, the tendency of the more widely read commentators in the inter-war years was to establish a broad identity between the Classical School and the propagation of *laissez-faire* doctrine. Alexander Gray, for example, described Adam Smith as 'the great apostle of *laissez-faire*',[13] and Charles Rist similarly spoke of 'the *laissez-faire* doctrine preached by the school of Adam Smith'[14] (though he made clear the limits which Smith set to the application of the doctrine).

Even in the inter-war years, however, by no means all historians of economic thought were prepared to make this identification. Jacob Viner, for example, though conceding that Smith 'in general believed that there was, to say the least, a strong presumption against government activity', went on to state that 'Smith was not a doctrinaire advocate of *laissez-faire*'.[15] Marion Bowley devoted a chapter of her important study of Nassau Senior to a refutation of the popular view that the opponent of the Ten Hours Bill was an unqualified advocate of *laissez-faire*,[16] and her work is the more important in that it reflected a growing reaction to the traditional interpretation of the thinking not only of Senior but of the Classical School in general. This revisionist view emerged with full clarity in Lionel Robbins's *Theory of Economic Policy in English Classical Political Economy* – published in 1952 but based on a course of lectures given more than a decade earlier – in which he set out to demonstrate that the identification of *laissez-faire* 'with the declared and easily accessible views of the Classical Economists is a sure sign of ignorance or malice'.[17] Robbins's powerful indictment of the traditional view was taken up by a number of scholars, not least in the United States where G. J. Stigler and W. D. Grampp have lent their strong support to the revisionist case.

This changed emphasis was, of necessity, derived from a close study of the whole corpus of the writings of the Classical econ-

18

omists from Smith to Cairnes, and an appraisal of its validity would require a detailed examination of the texts which it would be as impracticable as it would be impertinent to attempt here. In broader terms the case of the revisionists may be said to rest, negatively, on the absence in the work of any of the major economists before John Stuart Mill of an explicit commitment to the principles of *laissez-faire,* and, positively, in the evidence of specific rejections of the application of the principle on the part of each economist. The validity of these arguments may be tested by brief reference to the work of some major members of the Classical School.

Among the Classical economists Adam Smith is not only first in time and in seminal importance but also most easily approachable in terms of description and analysis. His belief in the fundamental beneficence of the natural order enabled Smith to reconcile the idea of individual freedom with the pursuit of the general good and left him with 'a strong presumption against government activity beyond its fundamental duties of protection against its foreign foes and maintenance of justice'.[18] This commitment to *laissez-faire* was, however, moderated in two important respects. Because Smith set defence above opulence, the exceptions which in practice could be made to the application of *laissez-faire* principles were potentially wide and made explicit in relation to trade. Furthermore, Smith's ascription to government of the right and duty of 'erecting and maintaining certain public works and certain public institutions, which it can never be for the interest of any individual, or small number of individuals, to erect and maintain'[19] opened up possibilities of state intervention whose import can only be fully appreciated two centuries later. The public corporation and the nationalised industry, undreamt of by Smith or his immediate followers, are both assimilable within the explicit exception which Smith provided to his non-interventionist theory.

Ricardo may in some respects be not improperly described as the St Paul of the Classical economists. His debt to Smith is evident, but he diverged from his great predecessor at many important points. Ricardo shared Smith's belief in the existence of economic laws which it was the prime concern of the political economist to discover. In the *Principles of Political Economy and*

19

Taxation he set out 'to determine the laws which regulate the distribution' of the produce of industry.[20] Unlike Smith, however, Ricardo did not view the economic world as a mechanism working for the good of each and all of those who constitute it. His theories of wages and rent led him to the conclusion that the ordinary processes of economic development would only benefit the landowner; profits would be diminished and wages held to the level of subsistence. It was this analysis that made Ricardo appear a prophet of gloom to his contemporaries, and this was all the more the case since he saw no role for the state in remedying the natural deficiencies of the economic order. 'Wages', he said, 'should be left to the fair and free competition of the market, and should never be controlled by the interference of the legislature.'[21] Direful as might be the outcome of the normal operations of the economic system, there was nothing to be gained by interfering with them.

The view of Ricardo as a rigid advocate of *laissez-faire* is strengthened by a consideration of his attitude to two major controversies of his day. Ricardo's theory of rent led him to attack the protective duty on corn, and his theory of wages likewise prompted his opposition to the Poor Laws. Significantly Robbins, in his general defence of the Classical economists, takes his stand for Ricardo not in his chapter on 'The Economic Functions of the State' but in that on 'The Condition of the People'. The evidence that Ricardo was much more sympathetic to the needs and aspirations of labour than the taunts of his critics have sometimes suggested is strong, but such sentiments are not in themselves inconsistent with a general belief in *laissez-faire*. More to the point in indicating a limitation to Ricardo's commitment is a consideration of his attitude to questions of public policy. In part this is shown by his gradualist approach to the Corn Law and Poor Law questions. Even more is it revealed in his strongly expressed views in the monetary field, notably his proposal for a capital levy to repay the war debt after 1815 and his powerful advocacy of a strict government regulation of the note issue.

Malthus was Ricardo's contemporary and with him shared the doubtful distinction of earning for political economy the title of the 'dismal science'. Just as the belief that Ricardo was the propagator of *laissez-faire* derives substantially from his theory of

20

rent, so the identification of Malthus with the same doctrine is traceable to his exposition of the theory of population and his use of that theory to attack the Poor Laws. But those who see consistency of thought and policy as an essential ingredient of the *laissez-faire* economist must find it difficult to place Malthus in such company, for Malthus was guilty of the ultimate heresy of his own day in supporting first the introduction and then the continuance of a duty on corn designed to protect the interests of the agriculturalist.

With McCulloch and Nassau Senior, Classical economics advances a generation. When Ricardo died in 1823, McCulloch and Senior had still their most notable work ahead of them. Moreover, the material environment which inevitably influenced economic thinking was changing rapidly. The second quarter of the nineteenth century, a period of rapid economic evolution, was filled with major economic and social controversies. There were great continuing debates on protection, the factory question, the Poor Laws, the railways, the organisation of local government and education, and currency and banking. No economist could escape involvement in a multiplicity of controversies, and these in their turn brought to the forefront of debate the question of the role of the state both in particular situations and in terms of general policy. Where Ricardo and Malthus never made an explicit general statement on the interventionist issue, economists from McCulloch and Senior onwards were almost inevitably driven to do so.

The pronouncements of McCulloch and Senior on this issue, however, though clear in themselves, are not wholly consistent. Thus on one occasion Senior asserted firmly that :

the duty of the Government is to keep the peace, to protect all its subjects from the violence and fraud and malice of one another, and, having done so, to leave them to pursue what they believe to be their own interests in the way which they deem advisable.[22]

On another he maintained that :

many political writers have supposed that public intervention

21

should not be made, that the business of government is simply to afford protection. This proposition I cannot admit. The only foundation of government is expediency, the general benefit of the community. It is the duty of government to do whatever is conducive to the welfare of the governed. The most fatal of all errors would be the general admission that a government has no right to interfere for any purpose except the purpose of affording protection.[23]

Similarly, McCulloch combined a commitment to *laissez-faire* so strong on occasion that Jevons could refer to him as an 'over-dogmatic economist'[24] with the assertion that :

the principle of *laissez-faire* may be safely trusted to in some things but in many more it is wholly inapplicable; and to appeal to it on all occasions savours more of the policy of a parrot than of a statesman or a philosopher.[25]

Such divergences are to be explained rather than explained away. In the case of Senior, in particular, time would appear to be an important factor. Almost twenty years separate the memorandum to Lord Melbourne with its strong leanings towards *laissez-faire* from the lecture which no less strongly points in the opposite direction. In those twenty years Senior took a vigorous part in the controversies of his day, and no doubt experience served to modify and change his ideas about public policy. McCulloch's criticism of *laissez-faire* as a dogma also comes at the end of this period and is coincident with John Stuart Mill's movement towards interventionism in the later chapters of the *Principles of Political Economy*.

This suggestion of a basic shifting of position on the interventionist issue in the post-Ricardian period is reinforced by reference to the specific policy commitments of Senior and McCulloch. Senior is well known as the opponent of the Ten Hours movement and of the legislative proposals which flowed from it; he had little sympathy with trade unionism and, not surprisingly, his writings on the French Revolution do not reveal him as a friend of socialism. But he supported a policy of wide-ranging governmental intervention in the economic affairs of Ireland and

22

advocated state regulation of building and urban sanitation. Above all, in his major contribution to Poor Law reform he distinguished himself sharply from the extreme *laissez-faire* position of Malthus and Ricardo.

McCulloch had different priorities of interest. Firstly and foremostly he became known as a free trader and a trenchant advocate of Corn Law repeal – though in the short run he preferred a fixed duty and a system of drawbacks to the total abolition of 1846. In his early years he identified himself with Malthus and Ricardo in seeking the abolition of the Poor Law, though with the passing of time he substantially modified this position. On the other hand, unlike Senior, McCulloch was tolerant of trade unionism and offered qualified support to the movement for factory reform; and he believed that the state had an important part to play in the development of transport. This extended to the right and duty of providing subsidies where private enterprise could not pay its way, and even involved the possibility of managerial commitment in the development of a railway system. Like Senior, McCulloch also accepted the principle of governmental responsibility for public health, with its implication of the necessity to regulate building and to supervise the provision of water-supply and sanitation.[26]

These deviations from *laissez-faire* opened up the way for the much more extensive and fully considered movement towards interventionism of John Stuart Mill. Unlike his predecessors for whom the question of *laissez-faire* had been at best incidental to the general discussion of economic principles, Mill set the role of government in the forefront of his argument. The fifth and final book of the *Principles of Political Economy* is given over to a consideration 'of the Influence of Government' and the last chapter of all to a discussion 'of the Grounds and Limits of the *Laissez-faire* or Non-Interference Principle'. So numerous and far-reaching were the exceptions to *laissez-faire* stated or implied in this chapter and elsewhere in Mill's later writings that some have placed him in the socialist camp and have found warrant for this in Mill's own assessment in the *Autobiography* published in the last year of his life.[27] The claim is in many ways exaggerated, but has sufficient substance to set in sharp contrast Mill's categorical affirmation in the *Principles* that '*laissez-faire* should be the general practice' and that 'the burthen of making out a strong case [rests] not on those who resist, but on those who recommend government interference'.[28] It is a matter for speculation whether Mill would have committed himself in this fashion had the *Principles* been written at the end of his life rather than a quarter of a century earlier; yet it is noteworthy that in seven changing editions of the work between 1848 and 1873 – the last appearing in 1871 – this cardinal passage remained unaltered and unannotated. Even the last great exponent of the Classical position, therefore, made no explicit renunciation of the *laissez-faire* principle, though the *Autobiography,* and the *Principles* considered as a whole, make clear how far he had drifted away from it in his prescriptive thinking.

This brief survey of Classical economic thought should at least suffice to dispose of the view, once frequently expressed, that the Classical School was a group of theorists rigidly committed to the principle of *laissez-faire*. In England only perhaps in the work of Herbert Spencer, by no means a major economic thinker, is it possible to find evidence to support such a thesis. But if it is possible to dissociate the Classical economists from the cruder versions of the *laissez-faire* doctrine with which they have been popularly identified, it is difficult to absolve them wholly from responsibility for fostering the *laissez-faire* idea. Even where the Classical economists did not positively embrace *laissez-faire,* they certainly showed no disposition to court its collectivist antithesis. To all, except perhaps John Stuart Mill in his later years, intervention was a necessary evil and every interventionist act needed its own specific justification.

The view of a basic commitment to *laissez-faire,* however modified its practical application, is borne out by a consideration of the seemingly paradoxical fact that, as the exceptions to a general policy of *laissez-faire* become more numerous in the writings of the Classical School, so their statements of adherence to the principle become more explicit. This apparent contradiction reaches its culmination, as we have already seen, in Mill; and it suggests the persistence of a strong undertow of *laissez-faire* thought and feeling in the intellectual world at a time when the

24

surface tide was beginning to run increasingly in favour of interventionism.

The dichotomy in the thinking of the Classical economists
explains in large measure the differing interpretations which contemporaries and later commentators have placed upon their
work. It is a contradiction, however, which is more apparent
than real and lies at least as much in the mind of the interpreters
as in that of the economists themselves. In order to understand
its origin and nature it is necessary to make a firm distinction
between the *analytical* or *diagnostic* and the *prescriptive* elements in the work of the Classical economists. The prescriptions
of the economists stand in relation to their analyses as politics is
related to political theory. Politics – the art of the possible – must
take account of factors and forces outside and additional to those
which constitute the data on which the theoretician builds his
ideal state, and likewise economic theory when related to the
situations of the common life must accept the tempering influence
of extra-economic forces. Jevons made clear this distinction
when he asserted that 'there may be general principles of nature.
So there may be general sciences of ethics, of economics, of juris-
prudence . . . But before we can bring the principles down to
practice they run into infinite complications and break up into all
kinds of exceptions and apparent anomalies.'[29]

The Classical economists contributed to the misunderstanding
of their own position by their failure to make a rigid separation
between their function as theorists, dispassionately analysing the
economic order and seeking to discover the laws on which it is
based, and their self-assumed responsibility as men of affairs pre-
scribing policies to meet particular economic situations. *Laissez-
faire* was not an economic law for the Classical economists analo-
gous to the laws of supply and demand, of population and of
rent. It was at best a principle or a rule, and as such falls in the
prescriptive, not the analytical, area of economic thinking; but it
was a prescription which in the minds of many followed logically and inevitably from the laws which the economists were dis-
covering and propounding.

Like all prescriptions derived from theory, however, *laissez-
faire* had to accommodate itself to the play of extra-economic
forces. It was the 'infinite complications' of a world in which man

25

was not solely an economic animal that led economists like Senior and John Stuart Mill increasingly to advocate policies whose object was, if not to influence the operation of economic laws, at least to moderate their consequences. Such policies necessarily involved state action on a growing scale. This is not to infer that the later Classical economists set aside the non-interference principle with impunity – quite the contrary. But every movement towards interventionism, however well considered and motivated, made it less easy to speak of a principle of *laissez-faire* and more necessary to talk in terms of a mere 'rule of practice'.

For some the prescriptive injunction not to interfere was so closely related to fundamental economic laws that it remained mandatory in virtually all situations. Those who like Spencer remained inflexible in their opposition to all intervention could justify their stand by reference to the basic theories of the Classical economists themselves; and it is significant that the economists – Ricardo and James Mill – who came to be perhaps most strongly associated with the *laissez-faire* doctrine were the two who most rigorously excluded the prescriptive element from their works of general theory. Interventionists, however, could also find warrant for their policies within the works of the Classical School, for, if the general theories of the economists still pointed strongly to *laissez-faire*, their specific prescriptions gave a no less clear justification for widening intervention. And when from the 1870s the old economic laws – and even the concept of economic law itself – became increasingly suspect, the interventionist case grew even stronger in proportion as the *laissez-faire* position was thereby undermined.

4 *The Transmission of Economic Ideas*

THE Classical economists were in no sense academic recluses –
though Smith, McCulloch, Senior and Cairnes were all at some
point in their lives holders of university chairs. Through the
Political Economy Club and similar institutions they mixed freely
with men of affairs – politicians, civil servants and others – and
took part in vigorous discussion of the major issues of the day.
Ricardo and John Stuart Mill were Members of Parliament, and
Senior, as a member of the Royal Commission, was one of the two
principal architects of the new Poor Law. All the major members
of the Classical School were active in publication, and all wrote
systematic general treatises on the new science of political economy. In their authors' lifetimes Smith's *The Wealth of Nations*
went through five and Mill's *Principles of Political Economy*
through seven editions, and a People's Edition of the *Principles*
had no fewer than nine printings between 1865 and 1873.
Ricardo and James Mill were less widely read – in Ricardo's case
no doubt because his style was as daunting as was his argument –
but McCulloch was a clear, lively and much read expositor of
Classical ideas.

Yet these immediate contacts were largely limited to a narrow
circle of the intelligentsia. The ideas of the Classical economists
reached a wider public through various secondary agencies, and
in transmission such ideas were inevitably subject to simplifica-
tion and distortion. The limitations and reservations which in
particular surrounded the concept of *laissez-faire* were set aside,
and through the writings of the popularisers and the preachings
of the propagandists the call to economic freedom and individualism became increasingly clear and insistent.

Among the vulgarisers of Classical economic theory Harriet
Martineau holds a position of undisputed pre-eminence. The
monthly sales of her *Illustrations of Political Economy* exceeded
10,000 in the 1830s whereas a decade later Mill's *Principles*
could only achieve a sale of 3,000 copies in four years.[30] When
Miss Martineau wrote, the influence of Ricardo was at its height.
Though in the *Illustrations* she never came out unequivocally in

favour of *laissez-faire,* the general tenor of her thinking lay clearly in that direction. John Stuart Mill, at least, had no doubt about it. 'Harriet Martineau', he wrote to Carlyle in 1833, 'reduces the *laissez-faire* system to absurdity by merely carrying it out in all its consequences.'[31] On the basis of her reading of Smith and James Mill – doubts have been expressed whether she ever came fully to grips with Ricardo himself – she became a strong advocate of free trade; from Malthus she took the theory of population and used it as a springboard for an attack on the old Poor Law; and similarly she employed the wages-fund theory to demonstrate the wastefulness and pointlessness of strikes. Though in their more extreme form her ideas might seem absurd to a John Stuart Mill, they made a ready appeal to many and 'helped to create that vulgar . . . image of the "dismal science" which passed for economic thought among the general public up to the 1870s'.[32]

The current of thought which was thus distilled from the early Classical economists by Miss Martineau, and which maintained its hold on the general public even while Classical theory was undergoing profound change, was reinforced from many directions. From its beginnings in 1843, at the time when the Anti-Corn Law agitation was approaching its climax, until 1859, when its founder and first editor, James Wilson, retired, the London *Economist* maintained an unqualified adherence to the principle of *laissez-faire. Laissez-faire,* as *The Economist* interpreted it, was wide-ranging in its application. It was as relevant to public health and education as to trade and industry and was based on a conception of a natural harmony of interests among humankind which far transcended even Adam Smith's optimistic assumptions. *The Economist* had a limited circulation – at most 3,000 – but it touched an influential segment of the upper middle class and found in that class fertile soil for the fuller propagation of its ideas.

The *Leeds Mercury,* under the editorship of Edward Baines and then of Reid, similarly emphasised the power of the inexorable forces of the market. As late as 1876, in reporting the meeting of the T.U.C. at Newcastle, a leader-writer in the *Mercury* was still referring to the 'survival of the old fallacious faith in the power of political institutions to arrest the action of natural

28

laws'.[33] The *Mercury* was a local newspaper of limited circulation, but among provincial journals it occupied a position of considerable influence and, like *The Economist,* gave rationality and coherence to opinions widely held among the industrial middle class. In this, if outstanding, it was by no means unique among English provincial newspapers of the early and mid-Victorian decades.

The London *Economist* and the *Leeds Mercury* were in a sense outriders for the Manchester School. The School is not to be simply defined : it was at once a body of doctrine, a powerful and highly organised movement for reform and a significant element in the growth of a great political party. Its ideas were derived wholly from the work of the Classical economists, but the derivation was selective. Smith contributed more than Ricardo and book IV of *The Wealth of Nations* most of all. As a movement for reform the School's first object was to end protection of trade, in particular the Corn Laws, and to destroy the remnants of the Old Colonial System. This pre-eminent concern for liberty in commerce supported a more general commitment to *laissez-faire* in economic matters, though Cobden at least was not opposed to factory reform. Through the teaching and still more the activities of the leaders and disciples of the Manchester School – Cobden, Bright and the Lancashire merchants and industrialists who lent their powerful support to the movement – the tendency for popular opinion to equate Classical economics with unrestrained economic individualism and advocacy of *laissez-faire* was accentuated; and this was the more important when the School, in terms both of ideas and persons, became a vital component in the emergence of the nineteenth-century Liberal Party.

It was especially through the Liberal Party that the ideas of the Classical economists found expression in Parliament. Ricardo had made his own contribution in the House of Commons between 1819 and 1823 when he had spoken with particular authority on the currency question. Senior, though not a Member of Parliament, had similarly brought a powerful influence to bear on public policy through his membership of the Poor Law Commission; and towards the end of his life John Stuart Mill also spent three years in the House of Commons.

29

But for the most part Classical economic thinking was expressed at Westminster in the speeches of many with little direct knowledge of the writings from which they drew their ideas. There has as yet been no attempt to make a systematic analysis of the debates of the House of Commons with a view to assessing the nature and extent of the influence of Classical economic thought in the mid-nineteenth-century discussion of public policy. D. H. MacGregor has pointed out that in the whole of the great debate on the repeal of the Corn Laws in 1846 *laissez-faire* was never mentioned in either House of Parliament.[34] Similarly, the investigations of W. O. Aydelotte into the division lists of the period of Peel's second ministry between 1842 and 1846 do not suggest the presence of any deep ideological division in the House of Commons at that time.[35] These are important observations, but it would be wrong to infer from them that ideology had no influence on the shaping of policy. When, for example, in May 1844 the Commons discussed the factory question on a motion tabled by John Roebuck, the debate did not contain a single explicit reference to *laissez-faire* but the argument was wholly about the non-interference principle.[36] Nor would it be correct to suggest that a belief in the virtues of *laissez-faire* was confined to a small group of individualist die-hards on the radical wing of the emergent Liberal Party. The influence of the Classical economists, and of the *laissez-faire* idea in particular, was widely pervasive in the House of Commons and not least in ministerial circles. Peel himself spoke in the factory debate of 1844, and two years later in a debate on the railway question he expressed his firm commitment to 'the great principle of permitting in this commercial country the free application of individual enterprise and capital'.[37] Such sentiments were widely shared in the House of Commons at the middle of the nineteenth century, and almost half a century later Gladstone was still expressing them before a now increasingly sceptical House. In every generation certain ideas tend to be assertive and to set the terms, if not to determine the final outcome, of debate. Such an idea was *laissez-faire* in mid-nineteenth-century England. It was, as Chesterton put it, 'the philosophy in office'.[38]

A parallel route for the transmission of ideas was provided by the Civil Service. Here the influence of economic ideas, though less pervasive, could be even more direct. The outstanding example is provided by the activity of John MacGregor, G. R. Porter and John Deacon Hume at the Board of Trade in the critical years between 1828 and 1841. All were convinced free traders in the full tradition of Adam Smith and through their work, particularly in the collection and deployment of statistical evidence, they exercised a powerful influence on the deliberations of the Select Committee on Import Duties in 1840 and on the commercial legislation of the succeeding decade.[39]

For the most part, however, civil servants in the established government offices lacked both the commitment and the opportunity to bring the new economic teaching to the service of policy. The case was different in those areas of public life where the problems of a rapidly changing society had brought new departments of government into existence – the Poor Law Commission, the Factory Inspectorate, the Railway Board and the Board of Health among others. Here the relationship between *laissez-faire* and interventionism made itself apparent in the work of men like Leonard Horner and Southwood Smith, but above all through the career of Edwin Chadwick. It was Chadwick, the one-time secretary and confidant of Jeremy Bentham, who, through his work at the Poor Law Office and the Board of Health, came to play so large a part in moulding the social administration of nineteenth-century England.

5 Benthamism, Laissez-faire and Interventionism

BENTHAM and his Utilitarian disciples are close to the centre of much of the current controversy about *laissez-faire* and state intervention in nineteenth-century England. To the economic historian this preoccupation with Bentham may seem somewhat excessive. It derives in part from the influential writing of A. V. Dicey, who identified Benthamism firmly with individualism and therefore was led to refer to the period of so-called Benthamite dominance between 1825 and 1875 as the age of *laissez-faire*.[40] For the economic historian, however, the idea of an age of *laissez-faire* does not finally rest upon a judgement of the validity of Dicey's analysis, nor upon an assessment of Bentham himself and of the contribution which he and his followers made to the development of economic and social policy in mid-nineteenth-century England.

Dicey was not the first, nor was he to be the last, to find a direct association between Benthamism and *laissez-faire* – though the association could not have been expressed more directly than in his assertion that '*laissez-faire* was practically the most vital part of Bentham's legislative doctrine'.[41] Harriet Martineau three-quarters of a century earlier had similarly related economic individualism to the principle of the greatest happiness of the greatest number[42] and, twenty years after Dicey, Keynes implied a similar identification when he argued that 'the language of the economists lent itself to the *laissez-faire* interpretation. But the popularity of the doctrine must be laid at the door of the political philosophers, whom it happened to suit, rather than of the political economists.'[43] Lillian Knowles and Fay each also stressed the relationship between the advocacy of *laissez-faire* and the propagation of the Utilitarian doctrine. Fay, however, made a distinction between the attitude of the Utilitarians to economic questions where 'the will of the manufacturers and the abstract laws of political economy' were to be given full play, and their attitude to social questions where a measure of paternalistic control by the state was required.[44] This distinction pointed the way towards an increasing realisation on the part of historians of the tendencies towards collectivism inherent in the Benthamite philosophy, and by 1948 Brebner had gone as far as to assert that Bentham was 'the archetype of British collectivism'.[45] Brebner thereby set the stage for a phase of the debate which has continued vigorously to the present day.

Discussion has been no less intense about the part played by the Benthamites in the so-called nineteenth-century administrative revolution in government. Where in the inter-war years historians had increasingly come to see in Bentham and his followers a major directing force shaping the form and content of Victorian governmental activity, a new generation began to question, not the collectivist implications of Benthamite ideology, but the influence which the Benthamites had exercised. While some pressed the claims of other movements of opinion working in nineteenth-century England, there was a growing preference for an organic rather than an ideological explanation of the forces making for increased government activity in Victorian society.[46]

The full discussion of these issues would be inappropriate in an essay which is primarily addressed to the needs of the economic historian, but even from this standpoint certain aspects of the wide-ranging Benthamite controversy call for attention. Three preliminary points require notice.

Firstly, Bentham lived for eighty-four years, and although his life was in many ways sheltered, his active mind could not but be influenced by the forces of change which were working so powerfully in England between the middle of the eighteenth century and the Reform Bill crisis of 1832. That on many issues he should have experienced changes of heart and mind in that period is not surprising and some of the apparent contradictions in his approach to the problems of the day were the reflection of a lively and responsive intellect adjusting itself to new ideas and circumstances.

Secondly, a distinction must be made between Bentham and the Benthamites. Benthamism – Utilitarianism, Philosophic Radicalism, the multiplicity of names emphasises the point – was not a highly developed body of rigid doctrine held in common by a tightly-knit and severely disciplined sect. Those who were called Benthamites were united in a shared respect for Bentham himself, in a common belief in the validity of the greatest happiness principle as a guide to social policy and action, and in a commitment to reason as the key to good government. As Dicey pointed out, Utilitarianism thus comprehended could in time be made the basis for many varied policies and systems spanning the entire spectrum from extreme *laissez-faire* to an all-embracing collectivism.[47] So long as Bentham himself was alive, the movement had a unity of action as well as of basic principle. After his death, its centrifugal characteristics became increasingly apparent in the lives of men so distinguished but so diverse as Edwin Chadwick, George Grote and the younger Mill.

Thirdly, it has to be emphasised that until at least the 1830s the Classical economists and the Utilitarians were united in both an ideological and a personal sense.[48] James Mill was at once Bentham's foremost disciple and a major economist of the Classical School. Through him a firm link was established between Bentham and Ricardo. Joseph Hume, active in the House of Commons between 1812 and 1855, was a member of the Benthamite circle who, though no profound economic thinker in his own right, yet maintained a consistent *laissez-faire* attitude to economic and social problems throughout all but the early years of his long parliamentary career. Above all Bentham himself, though rightly remembered primarily as a political philosopher and a law reformer, was a creative economic theorist not unworthy of recognition in the company of his contemporaries, Smith, Malthus and Ricardo.[49]

It is with his position as an economist that discussion can most appropriately begin of the controversies which have surrounded both Bentham and his philosophical system. Like other economists of his day, Bentham made a general obeisance to *laissez-faire,* more particularly when he stated his general rule that 'nothing ought to be done or attempted by government for the purpose of causing an augmentation in the national mass of wealth . . . without some special reason. *Be quiet* ought on those occasions to be the motto, or watchword, of government.'[50] But, more than Smith or Ricardo, Bentham provided numerous exceptions to his general rule – exceptions which mark him out no less as a forerunner of John Stuart Mill than as a follower of Adam Smith. The task of determining Bentham's precise standpoint on the *laissez-faire* question is made more complex by the fact that much of his economic writing was unpublished in his own lifetime, that his work in this field was virtually completed by 1804 when he had still almost thirty years of vigorous intellectual life ahead of him, and that even in the relatively short period in which he devoted his attention to economic matters he showed frequent changes of approach and attitude. It is not easy to go beyond the cautious conclusion that 'any attempt to pigeon-hole or classify Bentham is bound to be particularly misleading and any attempt at a precise and concise generalisation about his views on the role of the State especially hazardous'.[51]

In the long run, however, perhaps even more important than these ambiguities in Bentham's economic thinking was the fact that the followers of Bentham did not take their economic cue from their master. This was true even of Bentham's closest disciple James Mill, whose primary debt in economic thinking was owed to Ricardo. It was no less the case with Edwin Chadwick who, himself not an original economic thinker, drew his inspiration from the main body of Classical economic thought and most immediately from Nassau Senior.[52] With the death of Bentham such influence as he had directly exercised on the course of economic thinking largely disappeared, though his attack on the Usury Laws and his long-sighted views on taxation were praised by John Stuart Mill in the *Principles*.

The gap between the Ricardian economics of the Benthamite James Mill and the social engineering of Chadwick at the Board of Health is wide, though not perhaps quite so wide as Halévy inferred when he maintained that, while the economic thinking of the Benthamites rested on a belief in the existence of a natural harmony of interests, their approach to the wider problems of government and law was based on the contrary principle that government was needed in order to create an artificial harmony within the state.[53] This is controversial ground fought over by the big battalions – Halévy on the one side, Viner and Robbins on the other – and perhaps more the territory of the philosopher than the historian. The weight of the argument would seem to rest against Halévy,[54] but if at a fundamental level it can be demonstrated that Utilitarianism implied a positive rather than a natural interpretation of law in the economic as in wider fields, there remains unresolved the problem of reconciling the conflicting tendencies towards *laissez-faire* and interventionism which are discernible in Benthamite thinking.

This dichotomy, however, can be resolved at the level of historical experience. No Utilitarian believed in government for its own sake. What Bentham and his followers sought was not more but better government. In pursuing the greatest happiness of the greatest number they were seeking in the last resort not the happiness of a collectivity but the happiness of individuals; and if this end could be achieved without the intervention of the state, so much the better. For the Benthamites even the best government was a necessary evil. Much of Bentham's early effort as a law reformer was given to attempts to remove from the statute book archaic laws which seemed to restrict rather than to protect the life of the individual in society. This approach made him a friend of economic individualism and an opponent of legislation such as the Usury Laws which, he believed, was inimical to the welfare of the generality of individuals. It was the liberating qualities of the market economy which appealed most strongly to Utilitarian reason and sentiment in Bentham's own lifetime, and it was John Stuart Mill himself, later to be regarded as a harbinger of collectivism, who in 1833 declared that 'the [*laissez-faire*] principle . . . has work to do yet, work, namely of a destroying kind'.[55]

After 1830, however, in face of the increasing problems presented by industrialisation, population growth and urbanisation, the interventionist implications of the Benthamite philosophy increasingly asserted themselves. Foremost in their expression was Edwin Chadwick. But his was no conversion on the road to Damascus. Though his economic ideas became increasingly those of John Stuart Mill rather than of Ricardo, Chadwick never abandoned his adherence to the Classical economic system. Moreover, though their relationship is evident, a firm distinction must be made between Utilitarianism and Fabianism. Both can be comprehended within the terms of the greatest happiness principle, but whereas Fabian Socialists came to see the state as an agency acting positively to promote a greater good than individuals might achieve by and for themselves, the Utilitarians

36

always regarded the state fundamentally as a negative institution 'holding the ring' to prevent the war of man on man and to enable the individual to develop for himself the potentialities which lay within him. To this extent the Utilitarian contribution to the emergence of the Welfare State, however real, was essentially an unwitting one.[56]

Just how great that contribution was has been a subject of considerable debate. In the first half of the present century the view of Fay that 'the majority of essential reforms accomplished between 1820 and 1875 had the Benthamite impress upon them'[57] fairly reflected the general verdict of historians. This interpretation was based in part on a particular consideration of the emergence of the Factory Inspectorate, the reform and administration of the Poor Laws, the public health movement and the work of the Board of Health, in all of which, through Chadwick, the influence of the Benthamites was made evident. Those who in recent years have sought to minimise the Benthamite influence, either by advancing a different ideological interpretation or by propounding the thesis that all growth and change was basically organic, have likewise argued their case in terms of particular institutional developments – the struggle for factory legislation, the Passenger Acts and their administration, the Alkali Acts and other welfare legislation of the mid-nineteenth century.

The issues involved in this controversy are perhaps of greater significance to ideological and administrative than to economic and social historians. For the historian of ideas the relationship of ideas and events in the formation of policy is a theme as compelling as in the last resort its issue is indeterminable. If it is valid to suggest that without Bentham the reforming current of the nineteenth century might still have run its now familiar course, it may be claimed with no less plausibility that had there been no Bentham the nineteenth century would have had to create one. For administrative historians the issues, though more tangible, are no easier of solution. Older scholars may have claimed too much for the Benthamites; the revisionists have almost certainly allowed them too little. At the very least, it seems necessary to agree with Harold Perkin that though 'there were no doubt re-

37

forming administrators who had not read Bentham, and some perhaps – although it is very hard to believe – who had not heard of his name . . . those who had read Bentham, or talked to those who had, could travel all the faster for knowing where they were going'.[58]

See Thames 132.
See also Poor Law 1832.

6 Interventionism and Laissez-faire in Practice

THE view that the nineteenth century was an age of *laissez-faire* rests at the last on an analysis of the policies and activities of governments. In particular it has tended to be based on an examination of government policy in certain major fields of public concern. It is proposed to bring six of these fields under scrutiny. The areas chosen for investigation are important both in that they touched the interests of the community widely and deeply, and in that the discussions of policy brought sharp controversy into nineteenth-century political life. Two of the areas are essentially economic in character (free trade and the railways); two straddle the margin between the economic and the social (factory reform and Poor Law reform); and two are predominantly social (public health and education).

(i) FREE TRADE; THE RAILWAYS

The movement towards free trade can readily be – and has been – interpreted as the triumph of *laissez-faire*. For many, free trade came to represent *laissez-faire* in its purest form. The state could never, even if it wished, entirely extricate itself from involvement in the industrial life of the nation, but trade could be, and was, made free. The work of Huskisson, Peel and Gladstone was seen as a deliberate 'application of *laissez-faire* principles to our commercial system'.[59] This view is valid as far as it goes, but it is an oversimplification of the issues at stake in the free trade controversy. The achievement of free trade was the result of a combination of forces of which the ideological pressure for *laissez-faire* was only one. The interests of merchants and manufacturers, the demand for cheap food, the financial problems of government, the Cobdenite belief that free trade would open the way to world peace, and the changing balance of political power following the Reform Act of 1832, all contributed to the success of the free trade movement. Had these forces pointed not towards but away from free trade, the ideological claims of *laissez-faire* would hardly have sufficed to carry the day. *Laissez-faire* in commerce, as propounded most explicitly by Adam Smith and

McCulloch, gained its victory because it rationalised a course of action which the interests of the newly assertive mercantile and manufacturing classes and the exigencies of national finance were increasingly seen to require.

Before the end of the nineteenth century the conditions which had so strongly favoured the cause of free trade began to disappear. British industry came under increasing pressure from foreign competitors and for a period the export trade stagnated. It was these altered circumstances rather than a change in the climate of economic ideas which led to the emergence of Joseph Chamberlain's tariff reform policy and the movement of businessmen out of the Liberal Party. Two factors, however, served to delay the return to protection. The cheap food argument, rejected by the Chartists in 1846, proved wholly acceptable to a new generation of enfranchised working men sixty years later, and the growth of the export trade, halted for twenty years after 1875, was resumed with new vigour at the end of the century. Liberals like Lloyd George and Masterman, whose policies at other points indicate an approach far removed from *laissez-faire,* were at one with Cobden and Gladstone of an earlier generation in their belief in the necessity of free trade.

Though political reformers and free traders, with the triumphs of 1832 and 1846 behind them, might have thought otherwise, there is much justification for the view expressed by a commentator in 1851 that 'the most important event of the last quarter of a century in English history is the establishment of Railroads'.[60] Friends of *laissez-faire* welcomed the railway not least because its coming brought a challenge to the monopolistic position which the canal had established in many parts of Britain. But the advent of the railway, with all its technological, economic, social and administrative implications, presented Victorian governments with a host of problems and raised the interventionist issue in an acute form. The Classical economists believed in private enterprise and free competition. In general terms the one was regarded as the logical complement of the other. But what was to be done when private enterprise led to monopoly and as a result competition was extinguished? Adam Smith had made plain his intense dislike of monopoly, but he had not been presented with the

40

situation where choice lay between intervention and the passive acceptance of a permanent monopoly. However, on the basis of his clearly expressed view that the interests of the consumer should take precedence over those of the producer, it may be inferred that he would have thrown his weight on the anti-monopolist side.[61]

Smith's attitude was endorsed by later members of the Classical School, but it seems to have provided at best only limited guidance to politicians confronted with the problem of railway aggrandisement and amalgamation. The railway interest could appeal to the free enterprise principle in Classical economic thinking to support its desire to be free from state tutelage; those on the other hand who in the public interest wished to clip the wings of the adventurers could equally find in the writings of Smith and his followers abundant testimony to the evils of unrestrained monopoly.

When Peel approached the railway problem at the height of the speculative mania of 1845–6 he made plain the dilemma in which the government found itself as a result of the growth of this vigorous new form of corporate enterprise. After expressing his general adherence to the principle of giving full freedom to the play of individual enterprise and capital, he proceeded to use this principle to cover the activities of joint-stock railway companies, the terms of whose authorisation had implied the creation of 'a qualified monopoly'. In the affairs of such companies he would be 'unwilling, under all ordinary circumstances, to interfere'.[62] But the circumstances of the mania were such and the amount of speculative money involved so great, that he felt that the public interest compelled him to intervene.

The issue which presented itself to Peel in the peculiar conditions of 1846 became chronic as the railway amalgamation movement gathered strength. Amalgamation strengthened monopoly. Was it to be resisted on that account or accepted as the outcome of the normal operation of market forces? The problem, by no means always expressed in such stark terms of principle, was rarely far from the minds of successive Presidents of the Board of Trade in the years after 1846. The inconsistent policy which government and Parliament pursued in this period, sometimes accepting and sometimes rejecting amalgamation proposals, in

41

part reflected the dilemma. For example, a Select Commitee of both Houses in 1872 came close to concluding that amalgamation was inevitable and perhaps desirable; yet only a year later a major bill to amalgamate the North-Western and Lancashire and Yorkshire companies was rejected and another measure to bring together the Midland and the Glasgow and South-Western was also defeated. Though the nineteenth-century tide generally ran in favour of the forces of amalgamation, it was a tide of uncertain ebb and flow. It left Britain at the end of the century with a railway industry comparable only to mining in the degree of its regulation, yet no less distinguishable from the railway systems of continental Europe by the extent to which construction and management control was still exclusively concentrated in the hands of private enterprise.

(ii) FACTORY REFORM; POOR LAW REFORM

The railway amalgamation question, though its long-term social implications are evident, could be treated by governments primarily as an economic problem; free trade, more particularly in the emotive form of the demand for the repeal of the Corn Laws, was an issue with obvious social implications, but the humanitarian argument in favour of cheap food reinforced rather than contradicted the promptings of the economists. Like the Corn Laws, the factory reform question and the Poor Law were spheres of policy where economic and social considerations were both strongly in evidence, but in these areas the prescriptions of the economist did not necessarily accord with the programmes of the social reformer, and ideas of freedom of contract were seen in sharp conflict with notions of 'public morality'.

The view, once almost universally held by economic and social historians, that the Classical economists were opposed to factory reform, has come under sharp scrutiny in recent years. Historians of economic thought have always tended to be critical of it. Marshall defended the economists eighty years ago and more recently his assessment has been reinforced by the no less powerful advocacy of Schumpeter and Robbins. Two articles by K. O. Walker and L. R. Sorenson[63] add chapter and verse to this side of the argument. Yet it is possible that the pendulum has swung too far from the traditionalist view. Whatever may be inferred from the *dicta* of individual economists – and Senior and McCulloch, each of whom supported the Act of 1833, were both opposed to the Ten Hours campaign – it is evident that the general emphasis placed by Classical political economy on freedom of contract between master and man supplied an intellectual basis to which opponents of legislation could and did make appeal. As Mark Blaug has well expressed it: 'all things considered, the Ten Hours camp was not far wrong in regarding political economy with its slogan of "free agents" as a major obstacle to factory reform'.[64]

Against those who took their stand on the non-interference principle and rejected reform were men like Shaftesbury, Oastler, Howick and Carlyle who, while differing among themselves on many points, were at one in their rejection of what they conceived to be the tyranny of political economy. Out of the tension of these two forces, the one emphasising labour's function as an instrument of production, the other stressing the human needs of the labourer, there emerged in the Factory Acts of the 1830s and 1840s a policy which determined the form of such legislation for the remainder of the century. The Acts of 1833, 1844 and 1847 clearly represent a compromise. The principle that there should be no interference in the freedom of contract between master and man was honoured to the extent that no direct legislative interference was made in the relationship between employers and adult males; but the reformers gained the substance through the protection, provided by the law and enforced by the inspectorate, accorded to all women factory workers and to all, male and female, below the age of nineteen. The effect of this wide-ranging regulation of the hours of protected persons was in practice to impose a parallel restriction on the hours of adult male workers; but it was still possible to argue for a further half-century, if with diminishing plausibility, that the principle of non-interference remained inviolate.

Every piece of factory legislation involved some departure from *laissez-faire*. Yet the principle was not meaningless even to those who were active in the work of attrition which helped to weaken and destroy it. The speech made by Macaulay on the Ten Hours Bill in 1846[65] is important in its own right, but it has

43

added significance in that it reflected the attitude of many and not least of Peel himself.

> I believe [said Macaulay] that I am as firmly attached as any Gentleman in this House to the principle of free trade properly stated, and I should state that principle in these terms: that it is not desirable that the State should interfere with the contracts of persons of ripe age and sound mind, touching matters purely commercial. *I am not aware of any exceptions to that principle; but you would fall into error if you apply it to the transactions which are not purely commercial . . .* the principle of non-interference is one that cannot be applied without great restriction where the public health or the public morality is concerned.

In Macaulay's opinion there was no *economic* justification for legislative restriction of the length of the working day; such interference could only be justified in terms of the overriding *social* needs of a special category of workers who were incapable of entering into a proper contractual relationship with their employers. The argument is important in that, while it makes explicit the limitations to be set to the application of the *laissez-faire* principle outside the purely economic field, it affirms the paramountcy of the principle within that major area. *Laissez-faire* was unable to prevent the coming of factory reform, but for fully half a century it set significant limits to its scope.

The nineteenth-century history of the Poor Laws runs a not dissimilar course to that of factory legislation. However, while the nineteenth century created the factory laws *ab initio,* it inherited legislation deep-rooted in the Tudor past to meet the problem of poverty – legislation which had been designed to serve the needs not of an industrial but of a predominantly agrarian society. The theory of population as propounded by Malthus and endorsed by Ricardo pointed unequivocally to the abolition of the Poor Laws, and both economists in their prescriptions forcefully indicated the desirability of repeal.[66] But both felt that total abolition could only be achieved gradually. The reformers of the 1830s moved a step further in the direction of moderation. In that they sought to amend rather than to end the existing laws and in no way suggested that abolition was their ultimate aim, they were proposing and achieving a course which fundamentally ran counter to the prescriptions of Malthus and Ricardo and to *laissez-faire*. The measure of 1834, however, was essentially a compromise. Those who believed in the operation of a wholly unfettered market economy demanded the ending of all measures of relief : the reformers, on the other hand, sought to keep interference with the working of the labour market to a minimum. This they effected by the use of the workhouse test and the principle of less eligibility through which the living standard of the able-bodied pauper was forced down to the meanest level of subsistence. The corollary of this policy was that the Settlement Laws should also be liberalised, if not abolished, but in this the reformers of 1834 were less successful. Nevertheless, in that the expenditure on relief fell sharply after 1834 – the total amount spent had been £7 million in 1832 and it did not reach that figure again until 1868 – the Poor Law Amendment Act may be said not only to have achieved the immediate purpose of its inspirers but to represent a move in the direction of economic individualism; and, though in practice the rigours of the new law were gradually moderated, the principles underlying it survived into the twentieth century.

(iii) PUBLIC HEALTH; EDUCATION

Free trade and railway amalgamation were areas of policy where governments found it possible to shape their course almost wholly by reference to economic criteria. In the case of factory and Poor Law reform economic and social considerations each made powerful claims on the attention of the legislators and, since these interests were often in conflict, governments were forced into a position of uneasy compromise. Public health and education stood apart from free trade and the railways on the one hand and factory and Poor Law reform on the other in that social rather than economic interests were increasingly seen as paramount. In relation to both public health and education the interventionist tendencies of government provoked resistance, but in neither case was this primarily based on arguments in favour of economic *laissez-faire*.

45

The Public Health Act of 1848 was the fruit of much patient labour by a group of selfless reformers. To the historian living in a later century the Act now appears to have been a fragile instrument for the attainment of the major ends to which it was addressed; but contemporaries saw it as a powerful centralising force trespassing on the rights of elected local authorities. Many such authorities had come into existence as a result of the Municipal Corporations Act of 1835 and these were particularly jealous of their newly acquired rights. Such opposition to the authority of the central government may be seen as part of the general individualist movement of the nineteenth century[67] and to this extent can be regarded as one manifestation of the broad movement in favour of *laissez-faire*. There was even some resistance to public health measures *per se*. *The Economist* attacked the Public Health Act root and branch, opposing all legislation in this field, and twenty years later Herbert Spencer was still pursuing this theme. But neither *The Economist* nor Spencer could call upon support from the Classical economists. The public health question lay largely outside the economists' terms of reference; but convinced economic individualists like Macaulay and Samuel Smiles turned collectivist when the social issue of the health of the community was raised. Smiles, in particular, inveighed against *laissez-faire* when it was used to justify inaction in the public health field.[68]

Like the factory question, whose path it frequently crossed, education presented itself to nineteenth-century politicians both as an economic and as a social issue; but as time passed the social aspect tended to overshadow the economic. The subject was of continuing interest to the Classical economists, all of whom, except Ricardo, gave it an important place in their writings. They saw the education of the masses as a means through which the growth of population could be controlled; as a guarantor of social order; as an instrument of national economic development; and, not least, as an indispensable agent in the promotion of political democracy. To achieve these diverse ends the economists were prepared to accept large-scale intervention by the state. John Stuart Mill argued that governmental intervention in the matter of education was justified 'because the case is not one in which

46

the interest and judgement of the consumer are a sufficient security for the goodness of the commodity'.[69] McCulloch was if anything even more positive. 'Were government to interfere so far as to cause a public school to be established in every parish in England,' he wrote, 'its interference would be in the highest degree beneficial.'[70] There were some – none of them major members of the Classical School – who argued that the provision of education should be wholly regulated through the forces of the market economy. Adam Smith offered such views a modicum of encouragement when he expressed a preference for a system in which the expense of education was 'defrayed altogether by those who receive the immediate benefit of such education and instruction, or by the voluntary contribution of those who think they have occasion for either the one or the other',[71] but Smith was also prepared to recognise that education, being of benefit to society as a whole, could legitimately be made a public charge. The general view of the Classical economists was summed up by Mill when he asserted that 'Education is one of those things which it is admissible in principle that a government should provide for the people. The case is one to which the reasons of the non-interference principle do not necessarily or universally extend.'[72]

The controversies which surrounded education throughout the reign of Queen Victoria were not primarily concerned with *laissez-faire* in the narrower sense. The failure to achieve compulsory education before 1880, when Mundella's Act enforced school attendance on all children between the ages of five and ten, may be counted a victory for *laissez-faire*; but the notion is dubious because until 1870 at least compulsion was not considered so much 'undesirable' as 'unattainable'. The resistance to state control of education was more substantial, but the controversy was less about the justifiability or otherwise of central control than about the relative place in the educational system of the religious and secular authorities. John Stuart Mill, for example, expressed opposition to a system of state education. 'The government', he maintained, 'must claim no monopoly for its education. . . . It is not endurable that a government should, either *de jure* or *de facto,* have a complete control over the education of the people.'[73] But this was in no sense to imply that the state should leave education wholly in private hands. Mill was

47

scathingly critical of the education provided by the two great School Societies. It was 'never good except by some rare accident, and generally so bad as to be little more than nominal'. This was, in short, an area in which the *laissez-faire* principle in its economic sense had at best limited application. Once Parliament had made its first modest educational grant in 1833 the principle of interference had been established. From that point the question was not whether there should be intervention but what form that intervention should take and how extensive it should be.

★

This cursory view of six major areas of governmental activity in the nineteenth century indicates the strength and weakness of the *laissez-faire* principle. in its application to policy. The principle was all-pervasive; it is to be found as much in the discussion of education as of free trade, in the consideration of public health as of railway amalgamation. Yet while the claims of the non-interference principle could never be wholly excluded from ministerial calculations, decisions on policy often took an interventionist course. Even where the desirability of non-interference was conceded in principle, expediency demanded and secured policies which breached both the letter and the spirit of *laissez-faire*.

Historians who have argued against the notion of an age of *laissez-faire* have also drawn attention to a substantial array of new initiatives taken by government in the middle decades of the nineteenth century. Brebner, Holdsworth and Kitson Clark[74] all set out extensive lists of such interventionist initiatives undertaken in the years between 1830 and 1870. The lists, by no means wholly overlapping one another, impress as much by their range as by their length, though their emphasis is social rather than economic. The argument has been carried a stage further by David Roberts in his *Victorian Origins of the British Welfare State*.[75] Though Roberts is careful to stress the limitations both in conception and in achievement of the social legislation and administration of the Victorians, he sees in their governmental activities 'the first beginnings of the Welfare State which is today a distinguishing feature of the British Government'; and it is in pursuit of this same theme that Phyllis Deane has come to speak of 'a generation reared in the doctrines of *laissez-faire*' systematically laying 'the foundations of modern collectivism'.[76] The generation in question is that of the 1830s. The argument thus reaches its ultimate polarity, the age of *laissez-faire* coming face to face with the embryo Welfare State.

7 The Chronology of Laissez-faire

THE chronology of the so-called period of *laissez-faire* presents issues which are essentially subsidiary to and derivative from the main arguments about policy. Cunningham began his volume on *laissez-faire* with the publication of *The Wealth of Nations* in 1776, and ended it at 1850 when 'the reaction against *laissez-faire* had begun to make itself clearly felt, so far as the regulation of industry and of internal transport are concerned'.[77] Dicey, Cunningham's contemporary, identified the years between 1825 and 1870 as the 'period of Benthamism or Individualism' – the age of *laissez-faire*. Miss Deane, writing half a century later than either Cunningham or Dicey, saw *laissez-faire* as already in retreat by the 1830s.

These three examples make clear the diversity of view which obtains in this area of debate, though they by no means exhaust it. Miss Deane's 'age of *laissez-faire*' ends virtually at the point where Dicey's begins. Neither is coterminous with the period suggested by Cunningham. The more significant disagreements are those which relate to the date when the decline of *laissez-faire* may be said to be evident. Those who, like Miss Deane, see *laissez-faire* primarily as a destroying and purifying agency in society have tended to place emphasis on the period before 1830 when wage assessments were ended, the Statute of Apprentices repealed and the Assize of Bread abolished in London. Others, looking principally to free trade and to the restricted character of the social legislation enacted in the second quarter of the century, have viewed the years between 1830 and 1850 as the heyday of *laissez-faire*. Court and Hobsbawm, for example, both see *laissez-faire* ideas and policies as in the ascendent in the middle years of the century, and Hobsbawm speaks of a crumbling of the foundations in the 1860s and 1870s. This is not a new view. The notion that round about 1870 fundamental changes were occurring in British society which involved the replacement of an assertive individualism by a growing belief in and practice of collectivism has been propounded by British historians from the time of

50

Dicey onwards. Mrs Knowles, for example, maintained in 1921 that there was 'a striking contrast between the belief in the efficacy of *laissez-faire* which prevailed for the first three-quarters of the nineteenth century and the growth of State intervention and State control which have been the characteristic of the last fifty years'.[78]

In explanation and justification of this view, historians have pointed to fundamental changes occurring in the intellectual climate, in the body politic and in the economic fortunes of the nation in the years around 1870. It was at this time that some of the more cherished ideas of the older Classical economists were finally abandoned. In particular the labour theory of value gave way before the new theory of value based on the concept of marginal utility, and the 'new' economics of Jevons reinforced the revisionist tendencies of John Stuart Mill. In the related field of political philosophy T. H. Green, later to be followed by D. G. Ritchie, was giving a more positive role to the liberal state; and, more immediately and directly, the rise of an increasingly self-aware working class, given added influence by the Second Reform Act of 1867, was compelling both major political parties to reassess their social and economic policies. Behind these movements of ideas and men there loomed the fact of an economy under increasing pressure from new competitors in Europe and further afield – pressure which in time was to make even businessmen and manufacturers ready to question the validity of the *laissez-faire* principle both in industry and in trade.

To many, therefore, the period 1865–85 has seemed to cover the years when *laissez-faire* finally lost its dominance. Not all, however, have shared this view. Alongside those who have seen *laissez-faire* as already a dying force before 1860 are to be set many who have accorded it a much longer life. Even Clapham, for example, though he would have had no time for an 'age of *laissez-faire*' or for any other 'age', saw the Victorian state of the mid-1880s as little removed in its powers and pretensions from the state of half a century earlier.[79] The team of distinguished authorities who produced the Liberal Yellow Book in 1928 viewed the whole of the nineteenth century as an age of *laissez-faire*,[80] and J. M. Keynes in *The End of Laissez-faire* expressed a similar attitude. 'We do not dance even yet to a new tune. But a change is in the air.'[81] To some indeed the spirit of *laissez-faire* does not seem a spent force even in the 1970s.

The implications of these sharp divergences of view is clear enough. They reflect deeper divergences in the interpretation of *laissez-faire* and in the notion of what an age of *laissez-faire* implies. The agnostic, who rejects the concept of an age of *laissez-faire*, may well find in this conflict among the believers added evidence for his own unbelief.

8 Was There an Age of Laissez-faire?

WHAT continuing validity is there, therefore, in the notion of an age of *laissez-faire*? The answer must turn at least in part on the particular meaning which is attached to the term. The more rigid the definition and the wider the field of reference, the less plausible is the idea of an age of *laissez-faire*; the looser the definition and the narrower the area of application, the more justifiable does the use of the concept become. To give fuller content to this generalisation it is necessary to approach the concept of an age of *laissez-faire* through the eyes of four different types of historian – the historian of ideas, the historian of institutions, the social historian and the economic historian.

There can be no question but that *laissez-faire* played a major part in the thought-pattern of nineteenth-century England. Throughout the century a strong emphasis was laid on the rights and obligations of the individual. This belief in individualism, perhaps most clearly shown in Mill's *On Liberty* and Samuel Smiles's *Self-Help,* both published in 1859, was closely linked to the strong religious currents of the age. When *The Economist* attacked the Public Health Bill in 1848 it did so in the name of economic individualism but in words which invoked the religious spirit of the day: 'Suffering and evil are nature's admonitions; they cannot be got rid of; and the impatient attempts of benevolence to banish them from the world by legislation, before benevolence has learned their object and their end, have always been productive of more evil than good.'[82] *Laissez-faire* also readily attached itself to the Darwinian belief in the evolutionary process. Translated into economic terms, the message of *The Origin of Species* seemed to be that the progress of the race depended on freedom of competition in which success would go to those most fitted for survival and prosperity.[83]

But if *laissez-faire* can properly be assigned a prominent place in the fabric of nineteenth-century thought, it would be an exaggeration to suggest that it was the keystone of the arch. Such a thesis has more validity when considered in the narrower context of economic thought, but, as we have already seen, important reservations must be attached to it. Close scrutiny of the thinking of the Classical economists suggests that down to the death of Ricardo in 1823 the presumption in favour of *laissez-faire* among the leading exponents of the School was strong. Thereafter the doubts and reservations increasingly grew, though for half a century the belief in *laissez-faire* continued to be honoured at least in the letter. At a secondary level, however, faith in the *laissez-faire* prescription had both a stronger and a longer life; and it is in this respect that, from the standpoint of the historian of ideas, the notion of an age of *laissez-faire* may be said to have continued meaning.

It is hardly surprising that administrative historians have, virtually without exception, rejected the idea of an age of *laissez-faire*. A century which witnessed the rise of such institutions as the Factory Inspectorate, the Poor Law Board and the General Board of Health; which saw the work of men like Edwin Chadwick, Kay-Shuttleworth and John Simon; which experienced a growth in the size and quality of the Civil Service, assisted by, but by no means solely derived from, the work of the Northcliffe – Trevelyan Commission; a century in which in the view of some there took place a revolution in government comparable to that in sixteenth-century England : such a period is not readily to be described as an age of *laissez-faire*. In the course of the nineteenth century, government in Britain, faced with a variety of new and changing problems thrown up by the Industrial Revolution and the concomitant growth in urban population, became more efficient and professional and devised new administrative instruments to deal with new situations. The machinery of government, however, is the means by which policy is fulfilled, it is not policy itself. It was Dicey himself who asserted that 'sincere believers in *laissez-faire* found that for the attainment of their ends the improvement and the strengthening of governmental machinery was an absolute necessity';[84] and hence the rejuvenation of the Board of Trade under the stimulus of Porter, Deacon Hume and MacGregor was a major influence in promoting the cause of free trade.

It must be said, however, that means and ends – the machinery of government and the substance of policy – cannot always be held apart in this fashion. The emigration commissioners and the mines inspectors, creations of early Victorian England, represent not only new forms of administration but also new areas of government involvement in the life of the community at large. On the other hand, the Poor Law Commission, though its centralising tendency can be interpreted from one point of view as a departure from *laissez-faire*, was brought into existence to carry out policies which were inherently *laissez-faire* in character and had a direct effect in reducing the level of public expenditure. While it may be fairly conceded that the tendency of all governmental institutions is to be self-propagating, and that to this extent the administrative reforms of the nineteenth century made easier the extension of governmental authority, it also remains true that the persistence or decline of the *laissez-faire* ideal is to be judged primarily by the content rather than by the form of policy and administration.

It is therefore in the field of social and still more of economic policy that the idea of an age of *laissez-faire* can be most fairly tested. The earlier inquiry into six major areas of government policy ranging from trade to education has already provided some indication of the extent and limitations of the pervasiveness of the *laissez-faire* doctrine. It further suggests the broad generalisation that the more purely economic the area of governmental concern, the more strongly evident is the adoption of policies which can be legitimately described as *laissez-faire*. Conversely, where economic considerations are, or appear to be, subordinate, less weight is seen to be placed on *laissez-faire* prescription. This generalisation must not be pressed too far – Brebner, for example, has pointed to examples of state intervention in areas so identifiably economic as the laws relating to patents, bankruptcy, weights and measures and joint-stock companies – but in general there is warrant for the view that 'early Victorian collectivism was social and not economic in its emphasis'.[85]

Even in those areas of social policy, however, where state intervention was least inhibited by considerations of economic individualism, the limitations of governmental action are readily discernible. Intervention was prompted not by any conviction of its innate desirability but by the inescapable need to meet pressing problems, created largely by the twin forces of industrialisation and urbanisation, which were incapable of individualist solutions. The governments of early and mid-Victorian England did not so much seek to provide new remedies for old problems as to come to terms with the new crises which accompanied a rapidly changing social order. Although Parliament legislated widely and purposefully and the bureaucracy worked powerfully and at times heroically within the limits which successive governments set for it, Victorian social policy was basically negative and unconstructive. If the origins of the Welfare State are to be traced to the nineteenth century, the gestation period was long; in little over a decade the Edwardians accomplished more than the Victorians had achieved in two-thirds of a century.[86]

Such welfare services as the Victorian state provided were furnished at small cost to the central Exchequer. The average annual cost of the Factory Department within the Home Office at the middle of the nineteenth century was no more than £12,000, and the inspectors were being successfully induced to make still further economies. As late as 1870 the total expenses of civil government chargeable to the central Exchequer amounted to no more than £11 million, and less than half of this can be attributed to welfare in the widest sense. These figures, of course, relate only to expenditure by the central government, and in fact a large share of the burden of meeting the problems of a changing society was shouldered by local authorities in town and country. This preference for local rather than national action, subject to a minimum of central control, can in itself be regarded as one aspect of *laissez-faire*. But if *laissez-faire* is defined rigidly so as to exclude all public authority spending, whether national or local, the welfare activity of local councils inevitably becomes significant. Measured in financial terms such activity was undoubtedly growing perceptibly throughout the century, though at a much greater rate after 1890 than earlier.

In 1870 local authority expenditure in gross terms amounted to some 26s. per head of the population of England and Wales. Beside this can be set the 7s. per head of the population of the United Kingdom which was the sum spent by the central government on the provision of all civil services in the same year.[87]

Over the next twenty years expenditure both by the central government on civil services and by local authorities increased by some 60 per cent; and over the whole period from 1870 to 1914 the increase was fivefold in each sector.

In a qualitative sense the achievements and limitations of Victorian welfare policy are to be clearly seen in the Education Act of 1870. The Act was patently interventionist and implied a major extension of governmental authority in the educational life of the nation. But its limitations are no less evident and significant. Forster, in introducing his bill, declared the government's purpose to be 'to complete the present voluntary system, to fill up the gaps' – in short, not to attempt to improve upon or to compete with the work already being done by the voluntary societies, but to take up work which the societies had proved incapable of performing. Considered from this standpoint, the Act represented the antithesis of a belief in the virtues of public education in itself. If the voluntary societies had had the capacity to satisfy the total demand for elementary education, the Act of 1870 would have been as unwanted as it would have been unnecessary. Furthermore, in conformity with the strong deference paid to anti-centralist feeling in other fields of policy, the legislators placed the administration of the Act firmly in the hands of locally appointed School Boards. There is no evidence here or elsewhere in the wide area touched by Victorian social policy of that positive and affirmative belief in the inherent desirability of communal action – exemplified in the twentieth-century National Health Service – which is the hallmark of the Welfare State.

It is, however, in the area where social and economic considerations are seemingly of equal moment that the operation of the *laissez-faire* principle can perhaps be most interestingly investigated. Here the prescriptions of the economists pointing towards *laissez-faire* met the pressures of the humanitarians invoking state intervention; and the one tended to moderate the force of the other. The example of factory reform has already been investigated. If the admonitions of the non-interference school did not prevent the enactment of factory legislation, they at least restricted its progress and extent. The history of mining legislation runs a parallel course to that of factory reform. Ashley's Mines Act of

1842 – once described with a measure of exaggeration as 'perhaps the most high-handed interference with industry enacted by the State in the nineteenth century'[88] – forbade the employment of women and children below the age of ten in the underground workings of collieries. Its implementation was committed to the care of a single inspector. During the course of the next sixty years through the efforts of a much-legislating Parliament and a zealous inspectorate coal mining became the most intensively regulated and closely inspected of all British industries.[89] But except that in 1860 the minimum age for child labour was increased from ten to twelve, the legislature never again came so close to touching the economic nerve-centre of the industry, by interfering in the area of wages and hours, as it had done in 1842. It was not until 1908 with the enactment of the eight-hour day and three years later with the passing of the Minimum Wages Act that Parliament began to interfere directly with the internal economy of a great national industry. Yet throughout this period, by a wide range of regulations touching matters so various as the size of shafts and the appointment of checkweighmen, the legislature was not only paying increasing attention to the safety and welfare of the miner but thereby inadvertently – certainly by no conscious design – influencing the cost structure of coal mining. So finely balanced was the issue between economic *laissez-faire* and social intervention.

There remains for consideration the wide field of economic policy itself – that area where governmental decision was least trammelled by considerations of a non-economic, social or humanitarian character. Here *laissez-faire* solutions were most evident and most persistent. They were by no means universal, however. Peel, who at so many points adhered to the non-interference principle, preferred to speak of 'general rules' rather than of 'principles',[90] and was prepared, for example, to tighten the control of the state over the joint-stock banks and the banking system generally; and the overall effect of legislation in the wider joint-stock field may perhaps be regarded as interventionist rather than libertarian.

But in at least three major fields of policy governmental attitudes throughout most of the nineteenth century inclined strongly towards *laissez-faire*. Two of them – trade and the internal

58

economy of industry – have already come under discussion. The third no less important, is the economy of government itself.

Governments can influence the course of economic activity in a variety of ways : as consumers in the simplest sense (by purchasing battleships or bullets, provender for the royal stables or furnishings for the apartments of the judges); by special expenditure designed to stimulate the economy (e.g. through the establishment of public works); by taxation, variable in nature and extent and falling disproportionately on different sections of the community; by budgetary policy involving decisions to create surpluses or run deficits in the public sector; by the provision or withdrawal of credit through the banking system; and by a wide range of related expedients. All these may be, and in the present century have been, supplemented by the public ownership of important sectors of industry and by the control of industry through specific governmental instruments.

No government can remove itself entirely from involvement in the normal processes of a nation's economic life. All to a greater or lesser degree are consumers, all raise taxes and budget for their disposal. But above this minimal level the degree of governmental participation can be, and historically has been, enormously varied. In the nineteenth century British governments strove purposefully for the minimum : they abjured any right to direct the national economy. Their sole concern, expressed most cogently in the legislation repealing the Corn Laws and the Navigation Acts, was to make every element in the economy free to carve out its own path to prosperity. Gladstone's plea that money should be allowed 'to fructify in the pockets of the people' is well remembered because it expressed so clearly not only his own economic philosophy but that of all Victorian governments. Economy in public expenditure, long sought in the interests of the taxpayer, was now pursued as a policy virtuous in its own right.

Although government expenditure increased overall in the half-century between 1820 and 1870 – from £57·5 million to £69 million in gross figures[91] – virtually the whole of this increase took place as a direct consequence of the Crimean War, and the rate of increase was markedly slower than that of the growth of population or of the rise in the national income.[92] The bulk of this public expenditure was attributable to the cost of war, past, present or prospective, and as late as 1870, as has already been noted, the total civil expenditure of government amounted to no more than 7s. per head of the population, of which the charge for the administration of justice – internal defence – accounted for more than one-third. Though after 1870 government expenditure increased more rapidly, on the eve of the outbreak of war in South Africa in 1899 this growth was still doing little more than keep pace with the rise in the national income. It was only with the Edwardians that expenditure both on defence and welfare began to escape from the straitjacket in which Victorian parsimony had confined it.

The frugality with which nineteenth-century administrators expended their modest yearly incomes was matched by the care with which they raised them. Victorian budgetary policy had the single aim of balancing the annual accounts of the central government at the lowest possible figure. By twentieth-century standards taxation was highly regressive – though it would be wrong to see this as its primary intent. The Victorian system aimed at simplicity of assessment and collection and was designed to afford the minimum inconvenience to the taxpayer. Nor did the advent of free trade bring a sharp switch from indirect to direct taxation. In 1850 the reintroduced income tax only provided 10 per cent of government income; a further 8 per cent came from the land and other assessed taxes. On the other hand two-thirds of government revenue still accrued from the proceeds of customs and excise. Even in 1890, when on the one hand trade was at its freest, and on the other death duties had been introduced, indirect taxes still accounted for three-fifths of government income.[93] Much of this indirect taxation fell disproportionately on lower incomes – the excise on beer and tobacco, for example – and the income tax itself was not graduated except in the simple sense that all incomes under £150 were exempt.

Victorian governments, like the Classical economists, had no explicit theory of economic growth. But implicitly they believed that an economy thrives best when left to the free play of market forces. In this respect, therefore, the commitment to *laissez-faire* was positive, and the continuing expansion of the British economy throughout the nineteenth century seemed to validate this approach. The short-term fluctuations which produced both boom and slump, however, were accepted not as phenomena desirable in themselves but as the inevitable outcome of the operation of market forces. Nineteenth-century governments made little attempt to prevent or even moderate them and took only limited steps to mitigate their consequences.[94] It would be anachronistic to expect from Victorian governments a range of policies comparable with those deployed by governments in the second half of the twentieth century, but the essentially *laissez-faire* nature of the nineteenth-century approach stands out even by comparison with the expedients adopted by their predecessors.

The notion of an age of mercantilism is at least as suspect as that of an age of *laissez-faire* itself. There are problems about ideology, and the achievements of the politicians of the seventeenth and eighteenth centuries, in England as more generally in Western Europe, fell far short of their aspirations and intentions; yet the attempt to regulate the economy is as evident in this earlier period as is the deliberate abstention from such endeavour in the nineteenth century. Governmental economic policy in the nineteenth century had a different inspiration both from the policy of earlier generations and from the policy and achievement of government in the twentieth century. Though over a period as long as two and a half centuries such statistics have to be handled with particular care, it is evident that the upward movement of the level of government expenditure was much slower in the nineteenth century than either before or after. The growth of public expenditure in the eighteenth century – from £6 million to £16 million net in the fifty years between 1740 and 1790 – is largely attributable to the military needs of a nation which was more often at war than at peace; but, however explained, the increase represented a significant part of a relatively small national income. In the nineteenth century, once the French Wars were past, the relationship between the relative growth rates of national income and government expenditure was reversed. War, which so largely explains rising public expenditure in the eighteenth century, also played a large part in government spending in the twentieth, but a more than tenfold increase in real terms in the level of civil expenditure between 1900 and 1938 tells its own tale of the changing role of government in the

61

life of the ordinary citizen.[95] The marked changes in the relative amount of the gross national product attributable to government expenditure in general and to civil expenditure (including welfare) in particular are brought out strikingly in the following table:[96]

Government Expenditure by Function, 1792–1950
Percentage of Gross National Product Attributable to Government Spending (principal categories only)

	1792	1831	1850	1870	1890	1913	1938	1950
National debt and defence					4·0	4·5	12·9	11·6
Social services					1·9	4·1	11·3	18·0
Economic services					1·0	1·6	2·9	4·9
All services	11	16	12	9	8·9	12·4	30·0	39·0

By the late 1960s public expenditure accounted for over half the gross national product, and in its turn almost half of this was attributable to the social services and a quarter to economic services.[97] The changes coincided with the opening of the new century, but they gathered momentum after 1914–18 and still more after 1939–45. It was in this sense that Keynes could speak of the end of laissez-faire as taking place within his own lifetime. In these inter-war years there was a growing realisation of the part which governments could play in shaping the national economy; but it was not until after 1945, in part under the influence of Keynes himself, that peace-time governments came fully to accept their economic responsibilities and opportunities. The principles embodied in the budgetary and general economic policies of Cripps and Butler were far removed from those that had activated Peel and Gladstone. If the former may be said to have inherited the new world of neo-mercantilism, their predecessors may no less appropriately be said to belong to the age of laissez-faire.

It is therefore impossible to give an unqualified answer to the question 'Was there an age of laissez-faire?' Laissez-faire is in the mind of the beholder: it depends who he is and where he looks. One may, of course, take the viewpoint of T. S. Ashton who maintained that 'the whole practice of coining phrases and attaching them to particular periods of time has tended to cloud, rather than illumine, our vision of the past'.[98] The argument has undoubted cogency but at its extremes it tends to a type of historical nihilism. If it is conceded that phrases like the Renaissance, the Scientific Revolution and the Industrial Revolution are meaningful and helpful to the generalist and to a lesser degree to the specialist, the question remains as to what place in such company the notion of an age of *laissez-faire* can aspire.

The concept of an age of the Renaissance has validity because it is so wide-ranging in its applicability. Its centre of application may be the arts, but without strain it can be extended to the more general world of thought, culture and science, to the geographical discoveries, the crises in religion and the evolution of the nation-state. In short, the Renaissance touched the whole of the life of Western society. So, too, with the Industrial Revolution. Its heart is in the economy and technology, but its impact was on the whole of society, political and cultural as well as industrial and commercial.

It would be too much to claim a similar ubiquity for *laissez-faire*. To the political historian the notion of an age of economic freedom is certainly not an irrelevance, but like the historian of ideas he tends to see it as part of a wider concept of an age of liberty and libertarian principles, and for him the notion of an age of *laissez-faire* is confused by the coincident existence of an age of reform.[99] For the constitutional and administrative historian, *pace* Dicey, the idea of a period of *laissez-faire* has even less plausibility.

The notion of an age of *laissez-faire* must therefore find its validity, if at all, in the needs of social and economic historians – and this is as it should be, for it was among economists and with an economic connotation that the term first arose. For the *echt* social historian – a Hammond or a Perkin – *laissez-faire* is certainly a meaningful concept, and the notion of an age of *laissez-faire* is also valid in so far as it implies a period when *laissez-faire* ideas were powerful and influential in the formulation of social policy. But it would be wrong to infer from the use of such a phrase that there was a period in British history when social policy was determined by such ideas to the exclusion of all others.

As we approach the economic end of the socio-economic spectrum, the notion of an age of *laissez-faire* becomes increasingly easy to justify. The arguments in favour of this view have already been too fully rehearsed to need restatement, but in the last analysis they rest on a double base. On the one hand there is an inner coherence about policy, stretching from the theory of the economist to the practice of the politician, and on the other there is the powerful argument of relativity. It is an argument that has been expressed clearly by Viner when he maintained that:

> no social doctrine has a meaningful historical life except with reference, explicit or implicit, to an existent or conceivable alternative or array of alternatives. It is a useful simplification as a first approximation to regard the alternatives to *laissez-faire* as lying along a straight line measuring degrees of governmental intervention in the field of economic activity.[100]

Set beside the experiences and policies of an earlier and later age and related to the principles and practices followed by her European contemporaries, nineteenth-century England may be said to have come closer to experiencing an age of *laissez-faire* than any other society in the last five hundred years of world history.

This is, of course, not to imply that even in the economic field Victorian governments were wholly doctrinaire in theory or in action. Few governments are in principle and even fewer can be in practice. The applications of the non-interference principle to which Peel gave explicit assent had in each case to be tested by the question 'Will the practical good derived from any particular enactment in a particular case counter-balance the evil of that enactment?'[101] But the terms in which the question was formulated suggest the restrictive guidelines within which even Peel's empiricism had play, and Gladstone's self-defined terms of reference were no less limited. Thus, though *laissez-faire* was on more than one occasion honoured in the breach in Britain itself and still more clearly subverted in the economic policies applied to Ireland and India, it was until at least 1870, and arguably for a further twenty-five years beyond that, the strongest impulse influencing the shape and character of governmental economic policy.

Notes and References

1. For examples of the use of *laissez-faire* before 1850, see D. H. MacGregor, *Economic Thought and Policy* (1949) pp. 54 ff., and L. C. Robbins, *The Theory of Economic Policy in English Classical Political Economy* (1952) pp. 43–4.

2. Cf. also Lord Cromer : 'I have never accepted the view that a Free Trade policy means merely an absence of taxes imposed for protection purposes. . . . It means the support of individualism against collectivism.' Cromer to Bernard Mallet, 23 Feb 1910, quoted by Marquis of Zetland, *Lord Cromer* (1932) p. 323.

3. For a scholarly discussion of the nature of *laissez-faire*, see especially J. Viner, 'The Intellectual History of *Laissez-faire*', *Journal of Law and Economics*, III (1960).

4. L. C. A. Knowles, *The Industrial and Commercial Revolutions in Great Britain during the Nineteenth Century* (1921) p. 12.

5. J. S. Mill, *Principles of Political Economy*, ed. W. J. Ashley (1921) p. 950.

6. C. R. Fay, *Great Britain from Adam Smith to the Present Day* (1928) p. 368.

7. C. R. Fay, *Life and Labour in the Nineteenth Century* (1920) p. 48.

8. See D. Roberts, *Victorian Origins of the British Welfare State* (New Haven, 1960).

9. E. J. Hobsbawm, *Industry and Empire* (1968) pp. 190, 197.

10. See especially O. MacDonagh, *A Pattern of Government Growth: The Passenger Acts and Their Enforcement, 1800–60* (1961) and R. D. Collison Black, *Economic Thought and the Irish Question, 1817–70* (1960).

11. G. S. R. Kitson Clark, *An Expanding Society: Britain, 1830–1900* (1967) p. 162.

12. J. D. Rodgers, '*Laissez-faire* in England', in *Palgrave's Dictionary of Political Economy* (1910) II 535.

13. A. Gray, *The Development of Economic Doctrine* (1931) p. 142.

14. C. Gide and C. Rist, *History of Economic Doctrines*, 2nd English ed. (1948) p. 205. This widely read history went through seven editions in France and thirteen printings in English translation between 1915 and 1948.

15. J. Viner, 'Adam Smith and *Laissez-faire*', *Journal of Political Economy*, xxxv (1927) 219, 231.

16. M. Bowley, *Nassau Senior and Classical Economics* (1937) part ii, chap. i, pp. 237–81.

17. Robbins, *The Theory of Economic Policy*, p. 37.

18. A. Smith, *The Wealth of Nations*, ed. E. Cannan (1904 I 484 ff.

19. Ibid., ii 244.

20. D. Ricardo, *Principles of Political Economy and Taxation*, Everyman ed., p. 1.

21. Ibid., p. 61.

22. Memorandum to Lord Melbourne in 1830, included in the *Report of the Commission on the Handloom Weavers* (1841) p. 98 and quoted in Bowley, *Nassau Senior and Classical Economics*, p. 242.

23. N. Senior, *Lectures, 1847–52*, Course 1, Lecture 6, quoted by Bowley, ibid., p. 265.

24. W. S. Jevons, *The State in Relation to Labour* (1882) p. 9

25. J. R. McCulloch, *Treatise on the Succession to Property Vacant by Death* (1848) p. 156, quoted by Robbins, *The Theory of Economic Policy*, p. 43.

26. Cf. D. P. O'Brien, *J. R. McCulloch: A Study in Classical Economics* (1970) pp. 285–99, which gives an even more extensive list of interventionist proposals.

27. J. S. Mills, *Autobiography* (1873) p. 231.

28. Mill, *Principles of Political Economy*, ed. Ashley, p. 950.

29. Jevons, *The State in Relation to Labour*, p. 9.

30. M. Blaug, *Ricardian Economics* (New Haven, 1958) p. 129.

31. F. E. Mineka (ed.), *The Earlier Letters of J. S. Mill, 1812–48* (1963) i 152.

32. Blaug, *Ricardian Economics*, pp. 138–9.

33. *Leeds Mercury*, 23 Sept 1876. I owe this reference to Mr D. M. Jones of Leeds.

34. MacGregor, *Economic Thought and Policy*, p. 89.

35. W. O. Aydelotte, 'The Conservative and Radical Interpretations of Early Victorian Social Legislation', *Victorian Studies*, xi (1967) 225–36.

36. *Hansard*, House of Commons, 3 May 1844.

37. Ibid., 23 Apr 1846.

38. H. M. Lynd, *England in the Eighteen-eighties* (New York, 1945) p. 15.

39. Hume left the Board before the Committee began its sittings,

but he, like Porter and MacGregor, gave evidence before the Committee. See Lucy Brown, *The Board of Trade and the Free Trade Movement, 1830–42* (1958) *passim.*

40. A. V. Dicey, *Lectures in the Relation between Law and Public Opinion in England during the Nineteenth Century* (1905; 2nd ed., 1914) esp. Lecture VI.

41. Ibid., p. 147.

42. H. Martineau, *Illustrations of Political Economy* (1832–4) ix 144.

43. J. M. Keynes, *The End of Laissez-faire* (1926) p. 18.

44. Fay, *Great Britain from Adam Smith to the Present Day*, pp. 367–8.

45. J. B. Brebner, 'Laissez-faire and State Intervention in Nineteenth-century Britain', *Journal of Economic History*, viii (1948) 61.

46. For references see the bibliography, especially under Mac-Donagh, Parris and Hart. For a summary exposition of the issues and arguments involved, see V. Cromwell, 'Interpretations of Nineteenth-century Administration : An Analysis', *Victorian Studies*, ix (1966) 245–55. Among those who reject an ideological interpretation of administrative reform there are wide varieties of approach, e.g. MacDonagh establishes his own model of government growth (O. MacDonagh, 'The Nineteenth-century Revolution in Government : A Reappraisal', *Historical Journal*, i (1958) 52–67, esp. 58–61); Kitson Clark simply observes that 'it was the work of individuals reacting as best they might to particular problems and situations' (Kitson Clark, *An Expanding Society*, p. 147).

47. Dicey, *Law and Public Opinion*, Lecture IX, pp. 303–10.

48. Cf. Fay, *Great Britain from Adam Smith to the Present Day*, p. 368 : 'The political economists were Benthamites.'

49. Cf. Robbins, *The Theory of Economic Policy*, p. 2 : 'Bentham [was] much more important as an economist than is often recognised.'

50. J. Bentham, *Institute of Political Economy* (1801–4), in W. Stark (ed.), *Jeremy Bentham's Economic Writings* (1954) iii 333. This new edition contains a substantial introductory essay on Bentham's economic writings. The older 1843 edition of Bentham's works by Bowring is selective and has in the past created a misleading impression of Bentham's ideas.

51. T. W. Hutchison, 'Bentham as an Economist', *Economic Journal*, lxvi (1956) 301.

52. Bowley, *Nassau Senior and Classical Economics*, p. 274.

53. E. Halévy, *The Growth of Philosophic Radicalism*, trans. M. Morris (1928) *passim*.

54. See J. Viner, 'Bentham and J. S. Mill : The Utilitarian Background', *American Economic Review*, xxxix (1949) 368–9; Robbins, *The Theory of Economic Policy*, pp. 190–2.

55. Mineka (ed.), *The Earlier Letters of J. S. Mill*, i 152. Mill goes on to infer that *laissez-faire* is not a positive doctrine and that, once the work of destruction is completed, the principle will no longer have utility.

56. For further discussion of this point, see below, pp. 55–7.

57. Fay, *Great Britain from Adam Smith to the Present Day*, p. 367.

58. H. Perkin, *The Origins of Modern English Society, 1780–1880* (1969) p. 269.

59. W. Cunningham, *The Growth of English Industry and Commerce in Modern Times*, 3rd ed. (1903) p. 839.

60. W. Johnston, *England As It Is* (1851) i 260, cited by N. Gash, *The Age of Peel* (1968) p. 173.

61. Smith as an economic individualist and an anti-monopolist assigned a very limited role to joint-stock companies, but he felt that their existence was justified in the construction and operation of canals. He would therefore presumably have had no objection to the development of railways on this basis, but it is highly questionable whether he would have approved of the activities of a George Hudson.

62. *Hansard*, House of Commons, 23 Apr 1846.

63. K. O. Walker, 'The Classical Economists and the Factory Acts', *Journal of Economic History*, i (1941); L. R. Sorenson, 'Some Classical Economists, *Laissez-faire* and the Factory Acts', *Journal of Economic History*, xii (1952).

64. M. Blaug, 'The Classical Economists and the Factory Acts : A Re-examination', *Quarterly Journal of Economics*, lxxii (1958) 224.

65. *Hansard*, House of Commons, 22 May 1846.

66. 'This pernicious tendency of these laws is no longer a mystery since it has been fully developed by the able hand of Mr Malthus; and every friend to the poor must ardently wish for their abolition' : Ricardo, *Principles of Political Economy and Taxation*, Everyman ed., p. 61. There is some evidence that the extreme view expressed by Malthus in the *Essay on Population* was modified by him in later years.

67. Cf. J. Simon, *English Sanitary Institutions* (1890) p. 223 :

'At the present time there prevails a pretty general consent of opinion, that matters of individual interest are in general better cared for by individuals (separate or in combination or through elected representatives) than they can be cared for by officers of a central government.'

68. S. Smiles, *Thrift* (1875) p. 337.

69. Mill, *Principles of Political Economy,* ed. Ashley, p. 956.

70. *Quarterly Journal of Education* (Apr 1831), cited by O'Brien, *J. R. McCulloch*, pp. 345–7.

71. Smith, *The Wealth of Nations*, ed. Cannan, II 340.

72. Mill, *Principles of Political Economy*, ed. Ashley, pp. 953–4. The 'payment by results' system, introduced by Robert Lowe in 1858, may be said to have introduced the economy of the market into education, but it is of interest that the system was opposed by Herbert Spencer, the arch-exponent of *laissez-faire.*

73. Ibid., p. 956.

74. Brebner, op. cit., pp. 70–3; W. Holdsworth, *A History of English Law,* xv (1965) 17 ff.; Kitson Clark, *An Expanding Society*, pp. 147–62.

75. Roberts, *Victorian Origins of the British Welfare State*, p. 326. Roberts, however, points out that the work of the central government was frustrated by the play of 'localist and *laissez-faire* conditions' (p. 323).

76. P. Deane, *The First Industrial Revolution* (Cambridge, 1965) p. 215.

77. Cunningham, *The Growth of English Industry and Commerce in Modern Times,* p. 865.

78. Knowles, *The Industrial and Commercial Revolutions*, p. 117.

79. J. H. Clapham, *An Economic History of Modern Britain,* II (1932) 396 : 'As yet the sphere of the state had not greatly widened.'

80. *Britain's Industrial Future* (1928) p. 8.

81. Keynes, *The End of Laissez-faire*, p. 5.

82. *Economist,* 13 May 1848.

83. Keynes, *The End of Laissez-faire,* p. 14.

84. Dicey, *Law and Public Opinion*, p. 306.

85. Roberts, *Victorian Origins of the British Welfare State*, p. 95.

86. An exception may properly be made of the Workmen's Compensation Act of 1896, arguably the first Welfare State measure in Britain; but this came late and its impact was necessarily limited.

87. Of the moneys expended by local authorities, rather more than one-quarter was spent on poor relief. Of the moneys spent by the central government under the heading of civil government,

approximately 40 per cent is assignable to law and justice.

88. B. L. Hutchins and A. Harrison, *A History of Factory Legislation* (1911) p. 82.

89. Increased in numbers and capacity from 1850.

90. See the debate on the education of factory children (*Hansard*, House of Commons, 3 May 1844).

91. Based on B. R. Mitchell and P. Deane, *Abstract of British Historical Statistics* (1962) pp. 396–7.

92. Approximate growth rates, 1820–70 : gross government expenditure, 20 per cent; population (U.K.), 50 per cent; gross national income, 215 per cent. Based on ibid., pp. 396–7; 8–9; 366.

93. Ibid., p. 394.

94. But note the Poor Employment Act of 1817, which established a fund 'for the carrying on of Public Works' in instances where unemployment was high. The moneys involved were not large and did not substantially increase, but the provision persisted until 1875 and in a changed form thereafter. See M. W. Flinn, 'The Poor Employment Act of 1817', *Economic History Review*, 2nd ser. xiv (1961) 82–92.

95. Based on Mitchell and Deane, *Abstract of British Historical Statistics, passim.*

96. Data from A. T. Peacock and J. Wiseman, *The Growth of Public Expenditure in the United Kingdom* (1961) pp. 190–1.

97. *Public Expenditure: A New Presentation* (Cmnd 4017, 1968–9).

98. T. S. Ashton, *The Relation of Economic History to Economic Theory*, London Inaugural Lecture (1946), reprinted in N. B. Harte (ed.), *The Study of Economic History* (1971) p. 167.

99. Cf. the title of E. L. Woodward's volume in the Oxford History of England, *The Age of Reform, 1815–48.*

100. Viner, 'The Intellectual History of *Laissez-faire*', p. 46.

101. *Hansard,* House of Commons, 3 May 1844.

Select Bibliography

THIS subject has a very extensive and wide-ranging literature. The bibliography which follows is, therefore, selective. Where an author has written much on this subject, attention is drawn to the more important and typical writings. No attempt has been made to list basic works of economic theory. The works of Bentham (edited by Stark), Ricardo (Sraffa; also Hartwell), James Mill (Winch), Herbert Spencer (MacRae) and W. S. Jevons (Black) have all recently been the subject of new editions. For Adam Smith and John Stuart Mill the old editions of Cannan and Ashley respectively are incomparable.

W. O. Aydelotte, 'The Conservative and Radical Interpretations of Early Victorian Social Legislation', *Victorian Studies,* XI (1967). Uses parliamentary division lists of the 1840s to demonstrate the absence of any consistent ideological principle activating the social reform movements of the early Victorian era.

R. D. Collison Black, *Economic Thought and the Irish Question, 1817–70* (Cambridge, 1960). Important as showing the flexibility of Classical ideas in face of the problems of an underdeveloped economy.

M. Blaug, *Ricardian Economics: A Historical Study* (New Haven, 1958). A clear and invaluable exposé of Ricardian economics. Chap. 7 deals with 'Political Economy to be read as Literature' (i.e. the transmission of ideas) and chap. 10 with 'Matters of Economic Policy'.

——, 'The Classical Economists and the Factory Acts: A Re-examination', *Quarterly Journal of Economics,* LXXII (1958). Argues that the Classical economists tended to follow rather than lead the movement for factory reform and hence could not be regarded as 'the friends of reform'.

M. Bowley, *Nassau Senior and Classical Economics* (1937). An informed and critical evaluation of a seminal economic thinker and his relationship to the Classical system.

J. B. Brebner, '*Laissez-faire* and State Intervention in Nineteenth-century Britain', *Journal of Economic History,* VIII (1948), reprinted in E. M. Carus-Wilson (ed.), *Essays in Economic History,* III (1962). Stresses interventionist elements in

Benthamite ideas and in nineteenth-century thought and policy. At its time of publication a highly stimulating and provocative essay.

L. Brown, *The Board of Trade and the Free Trade Movement, 1830–42* (Oxford, 1958). Important study of the relationship between thought and policy.

W. L. Burn, *The Age of Equipoise: A Study of the Mid-Victorian Generation* (1964). An important general study, taking a broadly organic view of administrative change.

S. G. Checkland, 'The Prescriptions of the Classical Economists', *Economica*, n.s., xx (1953). A review of Robbins, *The Theory of Economic Policy* (q.v.), in which Checkland maintains that Robbins, in his zeal to refute real error, claims too much for the Ricardians.

——, 'The Propagation of Ricardian Economics in England', *Economica*, n.s., xvi (1949). Discusses, *inter alia*, the work of McCulloch and the Political Economy Club as agencies for the spread of Ricardian economic ideas.

——, *The Rise of Industrial Society in England, 1815–85* (1964). Chap. x relates economic theory to policy and broadly takes a traditionalist view. An important restatement.

J. H. Clapham, *An Economic History of Modern Britain*, 3 vols. (Cambridge, 1926–38). Chap. viii of vol. i, chap. x of vol. ii and chap. vii of vol. iii deal with the economic activities of the state at various periods of the nineteenth century. Has all the thoroughness and the abjuration of generalisation which is characteristic of Clapham's work.

G. S. R. Kitson Clark, *An Expanding Society: Britain, 1830–1900* (Cambridge, 1967). Argues (chap. 8) that the modern state had its origins in the nineteenth century and demonstrates the point by many examples of intervention between 1830 and 1900.

W. H. Coates, 'Benthamism, *Laissez-faire* and Collectivism', *Journal of the History of Ideas*, xi (1950). Sees a continuing relationship between *laissez-faire* and interventionist elements in Benthamite thinking.

A. W. Coats (ed), *The Classical Economists and Economic Policy* (1971). Editorial introduction by A. W. Coats. Reprints articles by R. S. Sayers, M. Bowley, R. D. Collison Black, M. Blaug, E. G. West, A. W. Coats and H. Scott Gordon. The Introduction is both informative and perceptive and tends to dissociate Classical economics from *laissez-faire*.

E. W. Cohen, *The Growth of the British Civil Service, 1780–1939* (1941, reprinted 1965). A useful sketch of the quantitative and qualitative advance of the Civil Service in the nineteenth century.

V. Cromwell, 'Interpretations of Nineteenth-century Administrations : An Analysis', *Victorian Studies,* IX (1966). Reviews the controversy about the 'nineteenth-century revolution in government' with particular reference to the part played in it by the Benthamites.

R. L. Crouch, '*Laissez-faire* in Nineteenth-century Britain : Myth or Reality?', *Manchester School,* XXXV (1967). Redefines *laissez-faire* to demonstrate that for the nineteenth-century economists and policy-makers '*laissez-faire* was more reality than myth'. An interesting against-the-tide contribution to the debate about economic theory.

W. Cunningham, *The Growth of English Industry and Commerce in Modern Times,* part II : *Laissez-faire* (1903). A seminal work, perhaps too lightly set aside in the recent past.

P. Deane, *The First Industrial Revolution* (Cambridge, 1965). Makes an interesting contrast with Knowles (q.v.). Chap. 13 emphasises the growing interventionist character of state policy after 1830.

A. V. Dicey, *Lectures on the Relationship between Law and Public Opinion in England during the Nineteenth Century* (1905; 2nd ed., 1914). Important and influential. Much criticised, on the whole deservedly, for the crudity of its generalisations and divisions; but its stimulating qualities survive.

C. R. Fay, *Great Britain from Adam Smith to the Present Day* (1928).

——, *Life and Labour in the Nineteenth Century* (Cambridge, 1920). Two much-read works of social history laying particular emphasis on the strength of *laissez-faire* ideas and the influence of Bentham.

S. E. Finer, *The Life and Times of Sir Edwin Chadwick* (1952). The standard life of the great reformer. Chap. 2 is particularly important for tracing the intellectual relationship between Bentham and Chadwick.

H. Scott Gordon, 'The London *Economist* and the High Tide of *Laissez-faire*', *Journal of Political Economy,* LXIII (1955). Traces the development and consistency of the *laissez-faire* argument in *The Economist* down to 1859.

W. D. Grampp, *Economic Liberalism,* vol. II (New York, 1965).

Sees nineteenth-century liberalism as essentially creating a mixed economy. Includes a perceptive study of J. S. Mill.

——, *The Manchester School of Economics* (Oxford, 1960). The most recent general survey of the ideas and work of the Manchester School, which Grampp sees as 'more an expression of middle-class radicalism than of classical economics'.

E. Halévy, *The Growth of Philosophic Radicalism*, trans. M. Morris (Paris, 1901–4; English translation, 1928). Like Dicey, a great authority who has been subject to recent criticism. His views on the intellectual basis of Utilitarianism and Classical economics are in part erroneous, but the book as a whole remains of high importance.

J. Hart, 'Nineteenth-century Social Reform : A Tory Interpretation of History', *Past and Present,* no. 31 (1965). A strong attack on the view of 'the nineteenth-century revolution' propounded by MacDonagh (q.v.). Reasserts in part the Benthamite interpretation.

E. J. Hobsbawm, *Industry and Empire* (1968). Contains (particularly in chap. 12) a lucid statement of the case for an 'age of *laissez-faire*'.

W. Holdsworth, *A History of English Law,* vol. xv (1965). An interesting and detailed statement from the standpoint of a constitutional lawyer of the rise and decline of *laissez-faire* in English policy between 1833 and 1875, as revealed in the enacted law. Argues that, while commercial policy was dominated by *laissez-faire* ideas, the principle was gradually abandoned in the interests of labour, the public and the state.

T. W. Hutchison, 'Bentham as an Economist', *Economic Journal,* LXVI (1956). A clear appraisal of Bentham's position among – and apart from – the main body of Classical economists.

J. M. Keynes, *The End of Laissez-faire* (1926). Particularly interesting as a discussion of the nature of *laissez-faire*.

L. C. A. Knowles, *The Industrial and Commercial Revolutions in Great Britain during the Nineteenth Century* (1921). An influential university textbook of the inter-war years.

R. Lambert, *Sir John Simon, 1816–1904, and English Social Administration* (1963). A modern biography of an important nineteenth-century administrator.

W. C. Lubenow, *The Politics of Government Growth: Early Victorian Attitudes toward State Intervention, 1833–48* (Newton Abbot, 1971). Based on four case studies. Argues against *laissez-faire* and Benthamite interpretations and in favour of a belief in gradualist adaptation.

O. MacDonagh, 'Emigration and the state : An Essay in Administrative History', *Transactions of the Royal Historical Society*, 5th ser. v (1955).

——, 'The Nineteenth-century Revolution in Government : A Reappraisal', *Historical Journal*, i (1958).

——, *A Pattern of Government Growth: The Passenger Acts and Their Enforcement, 1800–60* (1961). The major exponent of the organic growth thesis of administrative change in the nineteenth century. Minimises the role of Bentham and the Benthamites.

D. H. MacGregor, *Economic Thought and Policy* (1949). In chap. 3 advances arguments minimising the significance of *laissez-faire* in nineteenth-century social and economic thought and policy.

M. P. Mack, 'The Fabians and Utilitarianism', *Journal of the History of Ideas*, xvi (1955). Traces the relationship between Benthamite and Fabian ideas of society and the state.

R. M. MacLeod, 'The Alkali Acts Administration, 1863–84 : The Emergence of the Civil Scientist', *Victorian Studies*, ix (1965). A study in support of the MacDonagh thesis about the nature of nineteenth-century administrative reform.

B. Martin, 'Leonard Horner : A Portrait of an Inspector of Factories', *International Review of Social History*, xiv (1969). A study of the important and influential factory inspector who, though a disciple of *laissez-faire* in the economic area, saw its limitations when applied to the social field.

D. P. O'Brien, *J. R. McCulloch: A Study in Classical Economics* (1970). An important recent study. Emphasises McCulloch's interventionist tendencies in opposition to older views of his *laissez-faire* rigidity.

H. Parris, 'The Nineteenth-century Revolution in Government : A Reappraisal Reappraised', *Historical Journal*, iii (1960). An important riposte to MacDonagh's seminal article. His conclusion is 'that the nineteenth-century revolution in government, though not attributable to Benthamism as a sole cause, cannot be understood without allotting a major part to the operation of that doctrine'.

——, *Constitutional Bureaucracy* (1969.) Chap. 9 is a clear and well-balanced statement of the arguments about the 'nineteenth-century revolution in government'. Parris criticises both the Dicey and MacDonagh 'models' and argues that 'there was a nineteenth-century revolution in government, but there was nothing inevitable about it'.

——, *Government and the Railways in Nineteenth-century Britain* (1965). The most recent and much the best documented and argued treatment of its theme. Chap. 7 deals specifically with 'Railways in the Theory of Government'.

H. Perkin, *The Origins of Modern English Society, 1780–1880* (1969). A book of many parts with much that is germane to the *laissez-faire* question. Highly stimulating and well informed. Distinguishes perceptively between the entrepreneurial and professional ideals as stimulants to nineteenth-century policy and administrative evolution.

R. W. Prouty, *The Transformation of the Board of Trade, 1830–55* (1957). Independently reaches similar broad conclusions to MacDonagh. Has surprisingly little to say about free trade.

L. C. Robbins, *The Theory of Economic Policy in English Political Economy* (1952). A major revisionist study. Argues strongly and persuasively against older ideas which associated the Classical economists with rigid *laissez-faire* and repression of the labourer.

D. Roberts, 'Jeremy Bentham and the Victorian Administrative State', *Victorian Studies,* II (1959). Casts doubts on Bentham's influence on the development of the machinery of government.

——, *Victorian Origins of the British Welfare State* (New Haven, 1960). Important in seeing continuity as the theme of British social welfare history and finding Victorian (and pre-Victorian) origins for the Welfare State. Roberts is more cautious than some of his disciples, however, in setting limits to the scope and effectiveness of Victorian welfare provision.

H. Roseveare, *The Treasury* (1969). An important study tracing the emergence of the 'Treasury view' and also discerning Benthamite influences in its evolution.

G. de Ruggiero, *The History of European Liberalism,* trans. R. G. Collingwood (Oxford, 1927). Interesting as a study by a European intellectual. Sees *laissez-faire* as a major characteristic of English nineteenth-century liberalism.

L. R. Sorenson, 'Some Classical Economists, *Laissez-faire* and the Factory Acts', *Journal of Economic History,* XII (1952). Argues that the Classical economists were more favourably inclined to factory reform than tradition has suggested. This article has been criticised and largely superseded by that of Blaug (q.v.).

J. Viner, 'Adam Smith and *Laissez-faire*', *Journal of Political Economy,* xxxv (1927).

———, 'Bentham and J. S. Mill: The Utilitarian Background', *American Economic Review,* xxxix (1949).

———, 'The Intellectual History of *Laissez-faire*', *Journal of Law and Economics,* iii (1960).
The first and second of these are also in *The Long View and the Short* (Glencoe, Ill., 1958).
Three magisterial essays, defying adequate summary and indispensable in approaching this subject.

K. O. Walker, 'The Classical Economists and the Factory Acts', *Journal of Economic History,* i (1941). Limited to the period before 1833 and now largely superseded by Blaug (q.v.).

R. K. Webb, *Harriet Martineau* (1960). Biography of an important transmitter and vulgariser of Classical economic ideas.

———, *The British Working-class Reader, 1790–1848* (1955). A study of some aspects of the propagation of Classical economic ideas.

E. G. West, *Education and the State* (1965). Chap. 8 discusses the Classical economists and education.

C. Woodham-Smith, *The Great Hunger* (1962). Shows how British policy towards the Irish famine of the 1840s was conditioned by *laissez-faire* ideas.

Addendum

E. W. Cooney, 'Public Opinion and Government Policy in Nineteenth-Century British Economic History: a Review and a Study of the Building Industry', *Yorkshire Bulletin of Economic and Social Research,* xxi (1969). Concludes that 'building in Britain in the early nineteenth century was moulded decisively by the dominant [*laissez-faire*] economic dogma of the day'.

Index

79